Road Dogs and Loners

Road Dogs and Loners

Family Relationships among Homeless Men

Timothy D. Pippert

LEXINGTON BOOKS

A division of
ROWMAN & LITTLEFIELD PUBLISHERS, INC.
Lanham • Boulder • New York • Toronto • Plymouth, UK

LEXINGTON BOOKS

A division of Rowman & Littlefield Publishers, Inc.
A wholly owned subsidary of The Rowman & Littlefield Publishing Group, Inc.
4501 Forbes Boulevard, Suite 200
Lanham, MD 20706

Estover Road
Plymouth PL6 7PY
United Kingdom

British Library Cataloguing in Publication Information Available

The hardback edition of this book was previously cataloged by the Library of Congress as follows:

Pippert, Timothy D., 1970–
  Road dogs and loners : family relationships among homeless men / Timothy D. Pippert.
    p. cm.
  Includes bibliographical references and index.
  ISBN-13: 978-0-7391-1585-5 (cloth : alk. paper)
  ISBN-10: 0-7391-1585-5 (cloth : alk. paper)
  1. Homeless men—Interviews. 2. Homeless men—Family relationships. 3. Homeless men—Services for. I. Title.
  HV4493.P57 2007
  306.88081—dc22
                                                       2006027102

ISBN-13: 978-0-7391-1586-2 (pbk. : alk. paper)
ISBN-10: 0-7391-1586-3 (pbk. : alk. paper)

Printed in the United States of America

♾™ The paper used in this publication meets the minimum requirements of American
National Standard for Information Sciences—Permanence of Paper for Printed Library
Materials, ANSI/NISO Z39.48–1992.

For the fifty homeless men and women who took the time to openly share their experiences, hardships, and pain with me.

For Rob Benford, Lynn White, Helen Moore, Paul Amato and Sarah Fentress who provided guidance, support, and motivation.

For Caroline and Isabelle who provide me with a world full of joy.

And for Angela High-Pippert, who has done everything above, and more.

Contents

Chapter One

Learning from the Fight

The Fight

When the fight happened, I was not conducting research. In fact, I was simply serving lukewarm tuna casserole to about sixty homeless and near homeless men and women, as well as a few children, from a galley style kitchen with no stove or oven. I found myself serving tuna casserole in a daytime shelter, mostly out of guilt, but also out of curiosity. I knew that I wanted to study some aspect of the homeless lifestyle but I was uneasy about the ethical issues that are presented when researching vulnerable populations. Serving lunch helped to pave the way, both in terms of ethical issues and as an entrée into the field.

Examining the lives of the homeless means the researcher often becomes an uninvited intruder into the very limited personal space of a potential informant. The homeless typically spend a great deal of time in public space, not having a private refuge to retreat to, not having a door to close or a phone to hang up when a researcher is seeking study volunteers. Because of this concern, no research should be done on the homeless without a sincere attempt to give something back to this group or the organizations that are dealing with such issues. This philosophy led me to volunteer at a daytime homeless shelter for a few months before I began my research. Even after embarking upon my observational research and interviews with homeless men, I set a strict rule that for every hour spent observing or in an interview, an additional hour would be spent engaged in volunteer activities. In this capacity, I spent over three years serving in a number of roles. I spent countless hours preparing, serving, and cleaning up after lunches, sitting on the boards of directors for both The Living Room and Grace Kitchen, two agencies serving the homeless, and simply helping out with the daily duties of the shelter staff.

The Living Room, the only daytime shelter in a city of over two hundred thousand which was open and welcoming to homeless and near homeless individuals, was the obvious location to begin volunteering, and ultimately conduct research on the survival strategies and family relationships of homeless men. The drop-in shelter, one of the approximately forty thousand food, shelter, and service programs addressing the homeless problem in the United States (Burt, Aron, Douglas, Valente, Lee, and Iwen 1999), was fashioned around the concept of the community living room that was open to anyone as long as they were free of obvious drug and alcohol impairment. While there were a variety of services offered at The Living Room such as access to a social worker as well as laundry and shower facilities, its guests were free to simply play cards, read, nap, or socialize.

Even though the shelter was fashioned around a community living room, it did not resemble the living areas of middle class homes. First and foremost, it was public space that was only open from 7:30 a.m. until 4:30 p.m. The facility also did not look and feel like a warm and inviting living room as it consisted of a common room (approximately 40' x 30'), a kitchenette, the director's office, shower facilities, a storage room, and two restrooms. The common room was sparsely decorated with a magazine rack, eight long folding tables with chairs, a washer and dryer, and a counter used to place coffee and to serve meals. Despite the manager's attempt to keep the shelter clean, the smell of stale coffee, cigarette smoke, and soiled clothing could not be washed away.

The kitchenette area had little to offer. It resembled a galley kitchen typically found in efficiency apartments. The only appliances and cooking aids in the kitchen included a refrigerator, a microwave, a roasting pan, and a few cabinets sparsely stocked with cooking utensils and paper products. Forty to eighty persons were being fed breakfast, lunch, and a snack from that kitchen each day when I began visiting The Living Room. I was working out of that kitchen when the fight began.

While the center strived to present a welcoming environment, it could not escape the reality that it was filled with individuals that would not necessarily have chosen to spend their day with each other. This underlying tension, often exacerbated by a shortage of temp jobs or even an unseasonably hot or cold day, helped to sustain an atmosphere in which scuffles between guests were always a possibility. The shelter manager, Charlotte (all names and locations are pseudonyms), a very large and confident woman with strong tattooed arms and a stare that commanded attention, was able to keep most confrontations from escalating. Charlotte was also well liked and respected by most of the regulars, which meant that she always had someone who was backing her up, no matter how dangerous the situation. One of her fiercest supporters was Max, a recovering alcoholic who had spent time on the street but had recently become housed. He continued to come to the shelter, as he explained, to keep reminding himself why he needed to stay away from alcohol. Although Max did not have an official role at the shelter, he was usually helping Charlotte in some capacity. Having Max as an ally, especially when fights erupted at the shelter, was very advantageous. Max only stood about 5'7" but packed around two hundred fifty pounds of muscle, wore all black, and had a distinguishing tattoo under his left eye. No one ever challenged Max.

In the three years I spent volunteering and researching at the shelter, I came to see fights that were far more violent. In fact, at one point the shelter had to be shut down for a few days to let tempers cool down when non-English speaking Mexican men and those hostile to the newly arrived immigrants found it difficult to share the small shelter space. In a two day period during my second summer at the shelter, three guests were arrested stemming from a variety of racially motivated incidents. Outside the shelter a man was beaten with a lead pipe, a former Golden Glove boxer who frequented the shelter severely beat another guest, and a larger fight invoked a strong police presence in the days following the incident. But this fight was my first.

On an October day, one cooler than normal, a simple brushing of shoulders immediately turned into an all-out fight. Within seconds, all of the shelter guests had gathered around the two men who were fighting. The crowd encouraged them by yelling support and taunts as well as quickly rearranging furniture to allow for more room to fight. The quick spark and the proficiency in which the men fought made it more difficult for Charlotte to get a handle on the situation.

Even though I was volunteering, at my core I am a researcher and the situation proved too enticing to disregard. I glanced around the room and noticed that everyone in the entire room was involved in either watching or trying to support Charlotte in breaking up the fight. I was safe, or so I thought, to grab a pen and paper and begin taking some field notes. Who was fighting? How did it start? What role did the crowd play in escalating the fight? Why did the entire room erupt so quickly? How effective was Charlotte in breaking up the fight? When would Max step in to help Charlotte? These were all aspects of this situation that I did not want to forget. After a few minutes, Charlotte and Max had separated the men, kicked one of them out for the day, and were talking to the second fighter in a corner of the shelter. As quickly as the guests had thrown the tables and chairs to the side, they were returned to their places and the atmosphere was back to normal. If someone had walked into the shelter five minutes after the fight, they would likely have had no idea of the scene that had erupted only minutes before.

As I quickly resumed wiping down a table, I was approached by Rob, a man that had caught my attention prior to that day. I had never had a conversation with him but I had noticed him in the day room holding conversations with the other guests. He enjoyed telling his theories about the ills of society and how the system has wronged so many of the shelter guests. His conversations were typically so passionate, and in my opinion, intellectually sound, that it was difficult not to notice his presentation of self. He had also caught my eye because he did not seem to be homeless. He appeared to be in his sixties and certainly wore the physical signs of someone who has had a difficult life, but his clothes were typically clean and appropriate for the weather and he always looked to be showered and shaved. I later found out that he did have an apartment, but since retiring after forty years as a bartender, he did not have any retirement to speak of so he came to the shelter to eat. The food was not the only draw, however. He also came, as he explained, to watch people. After years of bartending, he missed the social atmosphere and The Living Room provided an outlet for him.

When he approached me, I became quite nervous. While a smaller and older man, he had a presence about him that seemed to garner respect from most shelter guests. My heart began to pound when he came so close to me that I could smell the coffee and tuna casserole on his breath. When he first spoke, his words nearly knocked me off my feet. He simply asked, "Are you a psychologist or a sociologist?" I stammered a moment while trying to think of an appropriate response, but all I could muster was, "What do you mean?" He stepped back a little bit, smiled at me, and said that he had noticed me taking notes during the fight. Obviously surprised, I tried to defend myself by telling him that I was sure that everyone was watching the fight. He said everyone was, except for him. He explained to me that he learned two life lessons after all those years behind a bar. His first piece of advice was never trust someone with tattoos on their hands. In his opinion, tattoos in general are fine but when someone puts them on their hands this symbolizes a crossing of a line, one that signifies a person who plays by their own rules and should not be trusted. This may be sound advice but so far I have not been able to use his wisdom in my daily life. The second bit of wisdom from his years as a bartender ultimately had direct ramifications for my research.

Rob's second piece of advice provided me with a research technique that I have utilized ever sense. Experience taught him that when everyone is watching an event unfold, in this case a fight, the most interesting place to focus your attention is not on the fight, but to look at what the observers were doing. Doing so led him to see me quickly turn from volunteer to researcher with the flick of a pen. And so he asked again, "Are you a psychologist or a sociologist?" I am a sociologist, and this book chronicles the research that began with a simple flick of a pen.

In the Beginning

My time at the shelter began in a much more mundane way about two months before the fight. As I walked into The Living Room, my notions about what I would experience were immediately challenged. My idea of what The Living Room would be like was based on "research" in front of the television and movie screen. I had not gone as far as envisioning a room full of bag ladies and tramps talking to themselves, but I had not expected a social atmosphere either. Because of this social atmosphere, despite the occasional fight, I was drawn to an investigation of homeless relationships. This study is an in-depth examination of how two subgroups of homeless men, loners and road dogs, negotiated family relationships and street partnerships. Road dogs, homeless men who tend to travel with partners, and loners, those who practice a more solitary existence on the streets, were compared in relation to their families of origin, families of creation (families developed by informants through marriage and/or childbirth or adoption), and fictive families formed between homeless men.

Often, when persons find themselves in financial or emotional trouble, the only alternative to "pulling themselves up by their bootstraps" is to turn to family members for assistance. Although many people see their family as persons who can be counted on in times of need, a considerable number of Americans are not able to rely on their kin. One group frequently unable or unwilling to rely on traditional family assistance is made up of those without permanent homes. For a variety of reasons, many homeless are unable, or refuse, to seek assistance from their families of origin. The reasons for limited emotional and economic support from families of origin include, but are not limited to, family separations, abandonment, death, institutionalization of children, chemical dependencies, financial instability, family violence, ineffective supervision and parenting styles, parent-child conflict, and a reluctance to ask for assistance. For example, several studies have found links between homelessness and those who had been placed in foster care, group homes, or other institutionalized settings (i.e., Courtney, Piliavin, Grogan-Kaylor, and Nesmith 2001; Sterk-Elifson and Elifson 1992; Susser, Struening, and Conovers 1987).

Created families are also a resource that most homeless cannot call upon or never developed. For many of the same reasons previously listed, separations, institutionalization, chemical dependencies, financial instability, etc., many homeless men never marry or raise children, and those who do so are unlikely to find such created families as a source of support. The absence of families of origin and created family ties significantly impacts the lives of many homeless persons, but the homeless face the loss of other ties as well. Baumann and Grisby (1988) explain that individuals are likely to go through three stages of loss before they become homeless. As we have discussed, the first stage of loss is typically the loss of family support, which is critical to an individual's social, psychological and economic wellbeing. The second stage of loss is the support from friends. Ties with friends are often severed, or at least extremely weakened, for the same reasons that ultimately rendered family ties unreliable or nonexistent. This is then followed by the third stage, loss of community support. Community support is frequently difficult to access, too meager, or unavailable to individuals with no permanent address, job, or means of transportation (Baumann and Grisby 1988). Once these ties are lost, or severely strained, life on the street does not make the establishment or maintenance of additional relationships easy. The homeless face multiple barriers in establishing interpersonal relationships, such as not being able to meet friends at the office, not being able to exchange addresses and phone numbers of those they meet, and often having no set schedules or reasons to meet others. As a result of the loss of previous supports, and the difficulty of developing new ones, homelessness has often been described as a condition of disengagement from society (e.g., Lafuente and Lane 1995; Bahr 1973).

Even though homeless lifestyles make relationship formation and maintenance difficult, the vast majority can and do establish relationships of significance. Despite the road blocks to relationship formation built into the homeless lifestyle, some relationships between homeless men and their families of origin and creation are maintained. Even when family members are not available to establish exchange-based relationships, many homeless frequently turn to other sources for support. Because strong family ties, friendships with the housed community, and community support are not accessible to many homeless persons, they are forced to achieve support by whatever means possible. What is available to the homeless is the friendship and assistance of other homeless individuals (McCarthy, Hagan, and Martin 2002; Kurtz, Lindsey, Jarvis, and Nackerud 2000; Dordick 1997; Sterk-Elifson and Elifson 1992; La Gory, Ritchey, and Fitzpatrick 1991; Grisby, Baumann, Gregorich, and Roberts-Gray 1990). In a study of one hundred fifty homeless individuals, La Gory et al. (1991) found that 79 percent had close friends and that around 60 percent suggested that their friends were helpful in their attempts to survive on the street.

There are many examples of relationships between homeless individuals that can be pulled from the literature (i.e., Kurtz et al. 2000; Dordick 1997; Wright and Draus 1997; Snow and Anderson 1993; Cohen and Sokolovsky 1989), but most of the research surrounding social relationships of the homeless examines extended networks or short-lived casual relationships. This study is unique as it focuses on two very specific subcategories of men found in the homeless community, loners and road dogs, and the different types of families from which they draw, or are unable to draw, support.

Road Dogs and Loners

Participants in the study were characterized by their willingness to form dyadic relationships with other homeless men. As such, informants were either classified as loners or road dogs. The terms road dog and loner are first-order constructs commonly known and used on the streets. Both classifications were based solely on self-descriptions. If someone identified themselves as a loner or as someone who would take another road dog, that was taken at face value.

Loner, as a first-order construct, was often used as an identifier during the interviews. For example, the phrase, "I'm just a loner" was offered repeatedly to explain a variety of situations ranging from whether they traveled with someone to how often, if at all, they called their mothers. At their core, loners were men who stuck to themselves on the street. They not only chose to sleep and travel alone the majority of the time, they typically accepted and offered little assistance to other homeless individuals. This did not mean that they lived in total isolation. Loners in this study as well as in other studies have been found to take part in group activities and even travel with someone on occasion. Still, such occasions are relatively rare and being able to trust others was frequently cited as an issue, leading to more isolation.

The term loner is certainly tied to multiple issues of mental health. Diagnosis of mental health disorders, or lack thereof, was not the focus of this study. Instead, self-classifications were used because how they defined themselves impacted their relationships on and off the street, and these relationships are the focus of this research. The topic of mental health problems, along with a greater discussion of the term road dog, will be addressed in Chapter Three.

The second classification of homeless men was road dogs. Road dogs are dyadic relationships between street partners, almost exclusively between two homeless men. Because road dogs tend to be male dyads, the study only focused on homeless men. Evidence from this study suggests that road dog relationships were commonly based on issues such as trust, reliability, and interdependence. Results also suggested that road dog partnerships lasted longer than most relationships formed on the street and practiced the sharing and exchange of resources helpful for survival. Like loners, being classified a road dog did not mean that the men always had a partner. Even those willing to take another road dog spent a great deal of time seeking food and shelter, as well as traveling, alone. Road dogs, unlike loners, were simply those who identified as being more open to traveling and seeking shelter with another homeless man when they found someone they could trust.

Furthermore, it was discovered that in a small number of these partnerships, some road dogs progressed to such a point that they saw, and referred to, their partner as a family member. Road dogs that have come to see their partner as a family member were referred to as lifelong road dogs in this study. Unlike loner, tramp, stiff, road dog and other terms used in this book, lifelong road dogs is not a street term. Regardless of commitment, traveling partners are called road dogs, but those who become family are believed to have lifelong ties, perhaps not in reality, but at least in theory. Because of the effectiveness of road dogs in providing the types of assistance usually furnished through family ties, and the possibility that road dogs may be formed as a substitute for absent family ties, the label fictive kin was used to describe these relationships.

Theoretical Framework

Homelessness is much more than the loss of a roof over one's head. Usually precipitated by some life altering events such as sudden unemployment, extended illness, family breakup, domestic violence, substance abuses, and a multitude of other hardships that are often beyond the control of the homeless individual, homelessness has an endless supply of serious precedents that accumulate over time. When a person eventually finds himself or herself on the street or in a homeless shelter, they have fallen so far from social and economic security that almost everything they once owned or could count on has been lost. In attempting to explain how the homeless men in the study dealt with such loss, three theoretical perspectives were drawn upon.

Three theoretical lenses were needed to explain the loss of contact with some family members, the maintenance of contact with others, and the creation of new fictive kin relationships. Gender theory (Ferree 1990) was utilized to address the meager level of support available to homeless men from their families of origin and creation by placing such relationships within a structure of gender constraints and expectations (Mennino, Rubin, and Brayfield 2005). Social exchange theory (Thibaut and Kelly 1959; Blau 1964; Uehara 1990) served a dual purpose and helped to explain relationships with families of origin and creation as well as road dog relationships. In relation to families of origin and creation, social exchange theory explained how exchange-based relationships were formed between some informants and their families as well as the multiple road blocks most informants faced when seeking such relationships. Social exchange theory also addressed the adaptation to the loss of traditional family relationships. When faced with few traditional sources of support, homeless often find support from their homeless peers (Kurtz et al. 2000; Sterk-Elifson and Elifson 1992) in order to better face the challenges of the street. Social exchange theory was adequate in explaining most such street partnerships because they were, at their core, relationships of trade and convenience. Occasionally road dog relationships progressed beyond arrangements of convenience and shifted to more complex relationships resembling kin. Such road dog relationships, referred to as fictive kin, were explained through the lens of new action theory (Scanzoni and Marsiglio 1993). Theoretical perspectives from the family and relationship literature must be part of this attempt to understand street partnerships because such ties appear not only to be based on reciprocity of goods, but also on the re-creation of family roles.

Gender Theory

In order to better understand exchange patterns between homeless men and their families, research on exchanges between housed men and their families were used to establish a pattern of gendered expectations for behavior. In addition to drawing from social exchange theory, gender theory was used to highlight the expectations placed on adult men in their capacities as siblings, sons, and fathers.

According to Ferree (1990), gender is the strongest predictor of behavior when examining the family-related actions of individual family members. Ferree (1990), however, does not advocate for a simple examination of behavior, but rather a focus on the categorization and stratification of gender. Utilizing gender theory allows the examination of family-level behavior, but requires the understanding that the examined behavior is often constrained and defined by gender. The strength of gender theory is particularly evident when examining adult child-parent relationships. When directly comparing adult children, parents have more contact with daughters than sons (Spitze, Logan, Deane, and Zerger 1994) and relationships between adult children and mothers tend to be closer than adult child-father relationships (Silverstein, Parrott, and Bengston 1995; White, Brinkerhoff, and Booth 1985). Eggebeen and Hogan (1990) conclude that women are more involved in exchange relationships with non-coresidential parents than are men. It was also discovered that the type of exchanges differed between men and women. Women were more likely to give advice and emotional support to their parents than men, and women were more likely to receive advice and childcare from their parents. They also found that women tend to receive more support than they give and men are more likely to be balanced in their exchanges with non-coresidential parents.

Examination of post-divorce families also indicates gendered patterns among relationships between parents and their adult children. Adult children with divorced parents report less contact (Booth and Amato 1994) and are less likely to engage in exchanges of practical aid (Amato, Rezac, and Booth 1995) and emotional exchanges (Umberson 1992) than their peers with married parents. It might seem obvious that diminished contact and support are a result of the divorce, but evidence suggests that gender also plays a role. For example, Booth and Amato (1994) contend that non-custodial fathers may be more likely to maintain contact with their sons than their daughters. Silverstein and Bengtson (1997) suggest that post-divorce mothers do a better job at maintaining relationships with their children, even in adulthood.

Indications that women are more likely than men to be involved in kin-keeping among relatives (Furstenberg and Cherlin 1991) can be used to address the actions of homeless men in the study. Such gender-based expectations serve as a baseline for what might be expected of informants. In short, expectations for exchange-based relationships between homeless men and their families should not be high given the constraints and liberties afforded men in family relationships. The expectations and actions homeless men had concerning their exchange-based behaviors, or lack thereof, with housed members of their families of origin and creation will be examined with a gendered lens in Chapter Six. A gendered lens, however, was not sufficient given the complex economic situation that constrained and necessitated social relationships. To complete the picture, social exchange theory was also drawn upon.

Social Exchange Theory

Social exchange theory describes the decisions to form, maintain, and dissolve relationships as basically a conscious balance of advantages and disadvantages (Thibaut and Kelly 1959). The process of gaining relationships is seen as a choice because it is believed to be a cost-benefit analysis in which emotional support, gifts, status, advice, money, help, compliments, and so on are exchanged. Blau's (1974) concept of social exchange also includes the flow of gifts, favors, etc. that are not negotiated and reciprocation is based on the discretion of the recipient. Such arrangements are based on the trust that over time exchanges will generally be balanced.

According to Caplow, social exchange focuses less on commodities that are transferred, and more on the "exchange of generalized personal willingness to respond to the needs of others, depending primarily on the degree of social relationship" (1984, 1315-16). Degree of relationship, as described by Caplow, can be based on kinship or as Blau (1974) explains, by an established pattern of exchange. When exchange relationships are applied to families, more leeway for unequal exchanges is often given. Rubin (1985) argues that there is a fundamental difference between friends and traditional kin. Kin, unlike friends, maintain a bottom line, referring to the fact that they can usually be counted on for material and service help even when a pattern of exchange has not previously existed (Rubin 1985). According to Rook (1987), the history of family relationships often allows for nonequivalent exchanges at any single point in time. Despite the possibilities for exchange, nonresident family members do not typically exchange at high levels. Hogan, Eggebeen, and Clogg (1993) estimated that half of Americans do not participate in exchange relationships with their parents.

While social exchange theory has been described as a powerful perspective through which to view the formation of relationships, it is not without limitations. One of the most constant and well-deserved criticisms is that social exchange theory is too simplistic and individualistic. For example, the basic premise of social exchange theory is that actors make rational choices about whether or not to exchange with another actor. Such narrow focus leaves no room for discussions of structural constraints such as economic conditions or social guidelines. In a study of homelessness, social exchange theory does not begin to address why informants are homeless and why they have little to exchange. While this is a legitimate criticism, the focus of this research was on the actions of actors when faced with many social and economic constraints. The goal of the study is not to explain homelessness or a lack of exchangeable resources, but how homeless men negotiated such circumstances. Some informants dealt with these circumstances by securing minor help from relatives while others lived the more solitary life of a loner. Others negotiated their situation by partnering with others in the same situation. The goal of examining such partnerships, road dogs, will be achieved by combining the strengths of both social exchange and new action theories.

New Action Theory

New action theory is a general perspective that takes a deconstructionist approach and recognizes that the traditional family is a socially constructed institution (Rice 1994). New action theory argues that families take on infinite forms and meanings (Scanzoni and Marsiglio 1993). New action theory can be beneficial to understanding street partnerships by allowing for the analysis of the ways in which homeless persons interact with others and cope with the social, political, and economic conditions that encompassed their lives. As applied to lifelong road dogs, new action theory was used to focus attention on the creativity of many homeless men in dealing with their general lack of resources and traditional family ties. More specifically, it allowed for the possibility that lifelong road dogs could be considered family, or fictive kin, based on the perspective of each partner and the actions performed by the dyad. The exploration of lifelong road dogs as possible fictive kin stemmed from, as well as contributes to, the debate in family sociology concerning family definition.

According to Scanzoni and Marsiglio (1993), there are four sets of interdependencies that give rise to perceptions of families: extrinsic, intrinsic, sexual, and formal. Simply put, extrinsic interdependencies include the sharing of economic, material, and other tangible resources. Intrinsic interdependencies deal with companionship, intimacy and other feelings and behaviors representing commitment. The third and fourth interdependencies, sexual and formal (legal marriage), are quite straightforward (Scanzoni and Marsiglio 1993). Obviously, all four interdependencies did not apply to lifelong road dog relationships, but extrinsic and intrinsic sets were pertinent. The connection was found in the acts of exchange and the interdependencies created when road dog relationships progress beyond simple economic ties. According to Scanzoni and Marsiglio (1993), the literature shows that a sense of being part of a family, or fictive family, can develop out of extrinsic and intrinsic interdependencies regardless of blood or legal ties.

New action perspective fits into the picture by allowing families to be viewed as social arrangements constructed by their members. By bringing the two together, we can take a step toward understanding how street relationships can move from a base of exchange to a fictive kin relationship. On the surface, new action and social exchange theories may not appear compatible. Because social exchange theory's roots are in structural functionalism and new action perspective stems from a postmodern framework, it may appear that they would differ too drastically to be used in tandem. This is not the case. Social exchange theory can be used to explain why relationships formed between homeless men. Street relationships are initiated based on the exchange of resources necessary for survival. New action theory allows for an understanding of street partnerships that progress beyond the initial stages of the relationship. It is a conceptual framework designed to focus on the struggles and adaptations of individuals in their everyday lives. New action theory is concerned with how actors negotiate, construct, and make sense of their opportunities. This negotiation and construction take place in the context of preexisting social structures. Because the homeless in the study typically had limited or no contact with housed family members and few material goods to exchange, an examination of this population pressed both new action and social exchange theories to their limits. Examining how road dogs used exchange to survive and how such acts occasionally led to more intimate relations where a renegotiation of family form took place is an exciting venue to call upon both perspectives.

In examining lifelong road dogs as fictive kin, it was not my intention to make the argument that these partnerships are as effective as family ties based on blood or law. In fact, the literature, as well as evidence from this study, suggests that these partnerships were very fragile and often short-lived. Despite the instability of these ties, I repeatedly found instances where they were very central to survival on the street. This study revealed partners that served as emotional outlets, housing brokers, protectors against violence and hunger, and other functions usually undertaken by family members. Additionally, lifelong road dogs were found who participated in such essential functions on a continual basis and who referred to their partners as family (i.e., "brother," "father," "he is my family," etc.). The partnerships of the homeless became fictive kin not simply because they provided means necessary for survival, but also because they were frequently the only bonds being formed. It seems possible that a weak substitute is better than no support at all. New action theory, social exchange theory, and gender theory are diverse lenses that were a challenge to bring together, but the complexities of informants and their relationships called for a varied approach. In pursuit of a greater understanding of the lives and family relationships of these men, these diverse family and relationship theories provided a greater understanding of the maintenance and formation of relationships available to homeless men.

Methodology

Because little is known about family ties among homeless men, this study was exploratory in nature and charged first and foremost with the goal of a detailed description of the family relationships and patterns of exchange among homeless men. Data were collected between 1997 and 1999 from two sources. First, and most central to the analysis, were in-depth interviews with forty-five homeless men. Secondly, thirty-five of the informants were given a self-administered survey measuring connections and support from family and friends (La Gory et al. 1991). The study investigated the roles different types of families played on the street. Specifically, homeless men who typically partnered up, took a road dog, were compared with homeless men who were self-described loners. These two groups were compared in terms of their contact and support with families of origin, creation, and fictive families formed between homeless men. A number of research questions were addressed in this examination of road dogs and loners. First, what were the physical, social, and economic conditions of the city's homeless community? Second, what type and level of exchange-based relationships were formed with families of origin and creation? Directly related to the second question is how homeless men adjusted to the absence of support from housed family members. The third and final area of inquiry examined what factors led to the formation, maintenance, and dissolution of road dog partnerships as compared to men who selected a more solitary existence on the street. Stemming from this question was the investigation of what constitutes a family, according to the respondents.

The Sample

The sample of homeless men was taken from the guests of The Living Room, located in Plainview, a Midwestern city with a population of over two hundred thousand. Shelter guests included the city's recent and long-term homeless, transient individuals, and housed persons with few, if any, resources or connections to the community. Due to the difficulty of distinguishing those who were homeless from those who were housed but relied on the shelter for meals and other assistance, probability sampling could not be employed. Instead, a purposive sample was acquired by utilizing screening interviews to assess if potential respondents were indeed homeless. Since the focus of the study included the formation of street partnerships, a purposive sample was used to select a greater number of road dogs while providing for a smaller comparison group of loners. Ultimately, thirty-three road dogs and twelve loners made up the sample of forty-five. In addition, the criteria for inclusion included men who spoke English and were at least eighteen years of age. Screening interviews, conducted at the shelter, typically resembled informal conversations with the potential informant to determine if they were currently homeless, if they considered themselves to be loners or if they had taken many road dogs, and if they were willing to participate in the study. Given the connection between loners and mental illness, care was taken to exclude any potential informants from the study that did not appear to be fully capable of voluntary consent. The overall response rate (87 percent) was excellent, with only seven men refusing to participate in the study. The most frequently cited reasons for declining to participate were that they were not interested, were on their way to a job, or had to meet someone.

Homeless women were not included in this study given the findings of a small pilot study. Five homeless women were interviewed to determine if they could be categorized as road dogs or loners. The interviews, as well as observational data, revealed that women and men typically had experiences on the street that were quite different. For example, women in Plainview had more services and programs available to them and were more likely to be traveling with created kin. During the two years of data collection, no street partnerships exclusively involving two women were observed. Street partnerships involving opposite sex partners were also more likely to be sexual in nature. These discrepancies would not allow for the direct comparison of experiences between homeless women and men.

Demographics

The sample resembled the general guests of The Living Room in that the majority were white, typically between thirty and fifty years old, and had varying levels of education. More specifically, thirty-eight respondents were White (84 percent), four Black (9 percent), two Hispanic (4 percent), and one American Indian (2 percent). A language barrier prevented a larger number of Hispanics from participating in the study. The mean age of the respondents was 39.51 ($sd = 8.74$) with a range of nineteen to fifty-four. The mean number of years of completed education was 11.56 ($sd = 2.3$). Fourteen respondents had not finished high school (31 percent), twenty-two had graduated from high school or obtained their GED (49 percent), six had attended college (13 percent), and three had earned a college degree (7 percent).

The level of created families among respondents is also of interest. Specifically, three (7 percent) were married at the time of the interview (only one was not separated). Sixteen (36 percent) respondents were divorced or widowers and twenty-six (58 percent) had never been married. Additionally, twenty (44 percent) respondents did not have any children, eight (18 percent) had one child, and seventeen (38 percent) had two or more children.

Interviews

In-depth interviews were employed to ensure that the research questions were addressed while allowing for a free exchange with informants. The interviews were designed as a series of friendly conversations, and a theme analysis (Spradley 1979) was used to analyze the interview data. The theme analysis allowed for an examination of both broad and specific themes. The end result was what Lofland and Lofland (1995) call a focused set of codes that emerged from the data. In the following chapters, textual accounts are used to demonstrate the focused set of codes and themes that have been generated.

The in-depth interviews were designed to assess each informant's family history, current family contacts, survival strategies, and propensity to partner up while allowing for an open flow of conversation. Most interviews lasted approximately forty-five minutes and took place in Grace Kitchen. Grace Kitchen was closed during the day so it provided a private space to conduct the interviews. Participation in the study did not lead to any major risks for the informants and was completely voluntary. Because the interviews were tape-recorded and transcribed, several steps were taken to ensure confidentiality. None of the recordings or field notes included the complete names of the respondents and survey results were matched to transcriptions by code. Once an interview was completed, the tapes were transcribed as quickly as possible and the contents were erased or destroyed. Before interviews began, informants were briefed about their participation and the IRB-approved informed consent form was explained. Informants were paid five dollars for their time.

Survey

After completion of ten interviews, a quantitative measure of support and contact was added to the study in order to underscore the interview data. Thirty-five of the forty-five informants were given, and completed, the survey (La Gory et al. 1991). Surveys were self-administered immediately following each interview. The survey assessed instrumental support from relatives as measured by the receipt of money, food, clothing, shelter, rides, advice, and healthcare. Contact with relatives in the past two months was also measured. The scale's reliability, measured by Cronbach's alpha, was .847 ($\overline{x} = 12.80$, $sd = 5.54$). Due to the limited sample size, data analysis was limited to simple descriptive statistics.

The Scope of the Study

Comparing road dog relationships with those who experience life on the street in a more solitary fashion sheds light on two approaches to navigating relationships among the homeless. This research contributes to the literature by pushing the limits of family definition as well as our knowledge of cultural adaptations and survival strategies. By focusing on homeless men, who are all too often isolated from their family, a great deal may be learned about how they coping with absence, adaptation to change, and creation of alternative relationships.

Policy considerations may also stem from this research. For example, because it has been found that many homeless survive by recreating families in pair bonds, homeless policies may need to address the necessities of the pair rather than those of the individual. In order to design a service delivery system for homeless populations, the social structures and help-seeking behaviors of these individuals must first be understood. If we know what people on the street must seek from others who also have limited resources, we know what services are not being provided. In addition, the experiences of informants who were able to maintain exchange-based relationships with family members could also be helpful. Determining why and how some men were able to maintain relationships with their families of origin and creation may help to explain these complex relationships.

In attempting to describe the lives and family ties of homeless men, the results of this research will be organized in the following way. Chapter Two sets the stage for the difficult task of categorizing homeless relationships. Included in this discussion will be summaries of the current debates in family sociology concerning family definition and the postmodern family. Chapter Two also includes a description of the general and Plainview homeless populations and then progresses to research focusing on relationship formation and dissolution. Chapter Two closes with an overview of fictive relationships within the homeless population. The fictive relationships of the homeless will be supported by an examination of fictive relationships found among prison inmates, African Americans, new immigrants and the elderly.

Results of the study are discussed in Chapters Three through Seven followed by a discussion of policy implication in Chapter Eight. Chapter Three describes the common and contrasting experiences of homeless loners and road dogs. Included in Chapter Three is a detailed description of the sample's demographic characteristics. Chapter Four outlines the family situations in which informants were raised. Special attention is given to levels of contact, support, and exchange-based activities between informants and their families of origin and creation. Chapter Five examines family background, contact, and support, for informants' created kin. The purpose of Chapters Four and Five is to provide detailed descriptions of the family ties and possibilities for exchange available to the sample rather than a theoretical examination of kin relationships. Chapters Four and Five furnish a baseline of support from which relationships between lifelong road dogs can be examined. The theoretical explanation for respondents' relationships with families of origin and creation, in terms of contact and exchanges of both tangible and intangible support, takes place in Chapter Six.

In Chapter Seven, the concept of lifelong road dogs is explored. Relationships between homeless men who partnered up for extended periods of time are studied in terms of patterns of exchange and the appropriateness of the label fictive kin. The extent to which social exchange and new action theories provide a better understanding of lifelong road dog relationships is assessed. Chapter Eight closes the discussion with a summary of findings and a discussion as to how the findings can be applied toward homeless policy.

Chapter Two

The Homeless and Their Relationships

The New Homeless

Homelessness is not a new issue in the United States. From its creation, the United States has been confronted by the problem of people who live on its margins, such as the homeless, the dependent poor, the unemployed, and the unemployable (Baum and Burnes 1993). Boston peace officers were charged with apprehending social outcasts or "vagrant persons" as early as 1640 (Kusmer 2002) and public emergency shelters could be found in the United States as early as 1796 (Jencks 1994). Although there have always been homeless in the United States, recent changes in government assistance and in the population's composition have led to a new view of the phenomenon. The political and economic climate of the 1980s contributed, at least in part, to an increase in the homeless population.

Since the 1980s the term "new homeless" has been used (Rossi 1990) to describe what is considered to be a population in flux. The "old" homeless are considered to be the older white men who frequented the skid rows of large cities in the 1950s, 1960s and 1970s. The new homeless are much more diverse, are more likely to spend time roughing it on the streets rather than skid row flop houses, include more women, minorities and children, are generally younger, have fewer resources, are more visible, and are a much larger population than the old homeless (Kusmer 2002; Smith and Smith 2001).

The difficulty of accurately defining and counting the nation's homeless, given the hidden nature of the population, provides for a wide range of estimates. For example, homeless advocacy groups in the 1980s were estimating that on any given night, two to three million persons were on the street when. According to Hewitt (1996) more accurate counts, ones not attempting to estimate those doubling up, put the numbers between three hundred thousand and five hundred thousand each night. More currently, the National Alliance to End Homelessness calculates that on any given night there are over seven hundred fifty thousand homeless individuals in the United States and between two and a half and three and a half million Americans experience a bout of homelessness lasting from days to months (2005). While specific numbers are debated, one aspect of the problem cannot be ignored, and that is that homelessness continues to grow. Increases in the need for emergency food and shelter have been documented each year since 1987, when the U.S. Conference of Mayors began recording requests in a survey of twenty-four major cities (2006). Estimates of the homeless population typically include those living on the streets, in cars, abandoned buildings, in homeless shelters, and in transition housing. Those not included are the millions of Americans who have doubled up with friends and relatives, those who are institutionalized, and those who are one unforeseen expense away from homelessness. "Homelessness, as measured in shelter counts or street estimates, represents but a fraction of the kinds of desperate circumstances in which our poor are housed. In some cities, for every 'officially' homeless person, there are several families doubled up or tripled up in apartments in temporary and makeshift arrangements" (Blasi 1990, 214). While these individuals may not be homeless at the moment, they are the population that cycle in and out of homelessness (Roman and Wolfe 1995).

Why are there Homeless?

The increase in the homeless population can be linked to at least four major factors. The most cited political and economic reasons for the increase in homelessness includes the absence of low-income housing, unemployment and low incomes, an aging baby boom generation, and the deinstitutionalization of the mentally ill. Jencks (1994) also adds the crack epidemic and the changing nature of family relationships.

Since the 1970s and 1980s, the supply of low-income housing has diminished, by half (Roman and Wolfe 1995). In 1994, almost ten million United States households were eligible to receive federal housing assistance but funding allowed aid for only four million (Roman and Wolfe 1995). According to Leonard and Lazere (1992), between the early 1970s and the early 1990s, 1.3 million low-rent units disappeared from the United States housing market. During this same period the number of low-income renters increased by 3.2 million. This period of time also saw average rental rates increase at rates much faster than average incomes. According to the U.S. Conference of Mayors (2006), this trend continues with 81 percent of cities in their study reporting increased requests for emergency shelter in 2005. McChesney (1990) likens the search for housing among the homeless to a game of musical chairs, with more people playing the game, and the fewer the chairs, the more people left standing when the music stops. As explained by Baum and Burnes (1993), the increase in the numbers of homeless can be blamed, in part, on the aging of the baby boom generation. In the same way that a population boom of seventy-six million people born between the late 1940s and the early 1960s crowded schools when they were young, there are now simply more persons in need of housing, at risk of becoming substance abusers, and mentally ill.

Not only can the increased number of baby boomers be connected to an increase in homelessness, but what happened to this cohort can also be cited. Cohort effects can be found in the fact that Vietnam Veterans are over represented among the homeless (Ropers and Boyer 1987). One reason that Vietnam Veterans are found on the street in disproportional numbers is likely associated with deinstitutionalization. More recent studies (i.e., Tessler, Rosenheck and Gamacne 2003) continue to find veterans overrepresented among the homeless.

Jencks (1994), Baum and Burnes (1993), and others contend that the deinstitutionalization of the mentally ill is also partially to blame for the increase in the homeless population. Between 1955 and 1985, the number of patients in state mental hospitals was reduced from 552,000 to 111,000 (Baum and Burnes 1993). Both of these factors, a rising middle aged baby boom population and a reduction in state mental hospital facilities, has created a situation where there is an enormous disparity between the number of people at risk and the public services available. Even many years after these changes, the lack of mental health services for impoverished youth and adults remains a significant problem (Kelly 2005).

While Baum and Burnes (1993) contend that deinstitutionalization accounts for a large increase in the new homeless, the roles mental illness and alcoholism play in the lives of the homeless is a hotly debated topic. Jackson-Wilson and Borgers (1993) estimate that about 30 percent of the homeless have substantial emotional or psychiatric problems. According to a synopsis of eight recent National Institute of Mental Health funded studies, between one-quarter and one-third of those homeless studied had serious alcohol and/or drug dependency problems (Tessler and Dennis 1992). More recently, the U.S. Conference of Mayors (2006) estimated that approximately 22 percent of the homeless could be considered mentally ill.

Baum and Burnes (1993) argue that some researchers underestimate the problem or simply avoid addressing these issues for fear that the homeless will lose public sympathy. Baum and Burnes point out that when examining drug addiction, alcoholism, and mental illness, somewhere between 65 and 85 percent of all homeless adults suffer from one or more of these conditions. "By refusing to acknowledge alcoholism, drug addiction, and mental illness as significant characteristics of the homeless population, we have failed the homeless. Instead, denial has let stand the age-old perception that people with these problems are the undeserving poor; and they have, in fact, been treated accordingly" (Baum and Burnes 1993, 24). No matter how you examine the numbers, substance dependency and emotional distress are problems that the homeless face in disproportionate levels. However, not all homeless or near homeless fit these descriptions.

The Homeless of Plainview

The Community Development Division of Urban Development Department of Plainview uses the following definition of homelessness:

> A person (youth or adult) or family who lacks a fixed, regular, or adequate nighttime residence and who has a primary nighttime residence that is:
>
> 1.   a supervised publicly or privately-operated shelter designed to provide temporary living accommodations including welfare hotels, congregate shelters, youth hostels, domestic abuse shelter, and transitional housing for the mentally ill; OR
> 2.   an institution that provides a temporary (less than 30 day) residence for persons intended to be institutionalized: OR
> 3.   a public or private place not designed for, or ordinarily used as, a regular sleeping accommodation for human beings (Urban Development Department 1996, 3)

Using this definition, Plainview's shelters (which included a battered women's shelter, a shelter for runaway youth, and the city mission), served approximately three thousand persons in 1996 (Urban Development Department 1996). Forty-nine percent of the population that had been served by the shelter system were men, 20 percent were women, and 31 percent were children under eighteen. Ninety-five percent of the male population was single (Urban Development Department 1996). In a separate Plainview study, 132 chronically homeless individuals were interviewed at emergency shelters, on the street, and at soup kitchens. Of those interviewed, 77 percent were male (90 percent of the men interviewed were single), 38 percent indicated mental health problems, 26 percent indicated substance abuse problems, 25 percent were military veterans, and almost 33 percent had been born and/or raised in Plainview. In the thirty days prior to the interview, the average number of days the respondents spent unsheltered was twenty-one days (Urban Development Department 1996).

To help secure an estimate of the population they served, The Living Room staff kept an unofficial count of all unduplicated persons who entered their facility. From April, 1998 to April, 1999, they served 1038 guests. Point in time counts in 2003 and 2004 demonstrate the continued problem in Plainview. In 2003, it was estimated that almost 1600 homeless persons, including those in transitional housing, were in Plainview. The estimate for 2005 was almost 2000 persons (Office of the Mayor 2004). These counts, however, likely missed many of the "hidden homeless," those living in cars, motel rooms, or staying with family or friends.

Another attempt to estimate the homeless and near homeless populations involved tracking the serving of meals. When the study began in 1996, The Living Room was serving less than fifty lunches each day and Grace Kitchen was serving less than one hundred dinners. By 1999, Grace Kitchen had taken over lunch service from The Living Room and the numbers for each meal regularly exceeded one hundred. By 2005, between three hundred and four hundred meals (lunch and dinner) were being served at the kitchen each day. Given that the kitchen served both the homeless and near homeless, the need for meals increased as the end of each month approached.

As indicated by the report from the Urban Development Department (1996), the homeless population of Plainview was not unlike those found in other cities. It was a population that could not be stereotyped as there are a variety of paths that have led to life on the street. Plainview was also like other cities in the fact that it lacked services available to single men. Plainview, a prosperous metropolitan area of over two hundred thousand, was large enough to attract a significant homeless population, as well have homeless from within its own ranks. The problem lies in the fact that Plainview was not considered by many large enough to need, or offer, adequate services to homeless men. I have said that Plainview is not "considered" large enough to offer these services because there appeared to be a general sentiment among city officials and community members that Plainview did not have a homeless problem, and if it did the city should not offer more services that would attract a larger problem. This is despite the fact that Grace Kitchen served over one hundred homeless and near homeless persons each day. Paradoxically, one reason many Plainviewites had the idea that there was no homeless problem in their city was because The Living Room was a place where the homeless and residentially at-risk could congregate during the day. The Living Room, like other day shelters, kept a large number of homeless off the streets of downtown, making the population almost hidden (Johnsen, Cloke, and May 2005).

I do not want to portray Plainview as not having any services available to the poor. Since 2000, public and private efforts to help the homeless have increased and even in the late 1990s emergency shelters, long-term and transitional housing assistance, and a variety of youth services could be found in Plainview. These services, however, were heavily targeted toward women, children, and individuals seeking substance treatment. There were residential substance abuse programs, places where a warm meal could be found, and men could be put on the long Housing and Urban Development (HUD) waiting list for housing assistance, but after sundown there were few places for single men to turn. Plainview did have a city mission and its presence was frequently touted as proof that Plainview is meeting the community's needs. The dynamics of the city mission, however, kept a number of homeless who were used to living independently from taking advantage of its service. For example, to stay at the mission you had to have your personal belongings locked up and under the control of mission workers and abstain completely from alcohol and other drugs. Mission guests also had to check in by 8:30 p.m. and be in bed by 9:00 p.m.

each evening. These rules proved to be too restrictive for most homeless men. Adherence to such rules helped to create a sentiment among the homeless who "roughed it" that those who stayed at missions, what Cohen and Sokolovsky (1989) identified as mission stiffs, were not "true homeless."

Insisting on complete abstinence from alcohol may be a practical way to maintain order. However, Don, a forty-two year-old Sally tramp (someone who frequently enrolls in Salvation Army programs while traveling but seldom finishes them), put the rule in a different perspective. Don described the following scenario of a time he attempted to stay at the city mission:

> I went out on a job when a guy came down to the mission and asked for a couple of guys to throw some hay. So we worked for him about three hours and made about $25.00. When we got done we cleaned up out in the yard...hosed down. The wife brought out a tray with some beer on it, a bottle of beer a piece. One beer! The farmer drove us into town. We got in late, about 8 p.m. The guy who was checking (at the mission) said he thought he smelled beer on my breath. They breathalized me. One beer got me kicked out for the whole night.

Even if one was willing to follow the rules of the mission, this was far from a permanent solution. While flexible guidelines allowed women and children to theoretically stay at the mission for years, unemployed single men were allowed a stay of three days. During that three-day period, the shelter guest must demonstrate that he was actively seeking employment. If this could be demonstrated, their stay could be lengthened to approximately three weeks. The only way men could stay for extended periods of time at the mission was to enroll in its religious program. Women and children were not required to enter the religious program in order to stay an extended period of time. Another limitation on the mission's ability to help was its size. The capacity of the mission was listed as forty-four men, plus twenty mattresses used for overflow. For women and children the capacity is forty-two persons, plus ten mattresses (Urban Development Department 1996).

Relationship Formation

As humans we spend the majority, if not all our lives, dependent on others. From the care of an infant by a parent to companionship in old age, dependency is a fundamental fact of the human condition (Berscheid and Peplau 1983). According to Powell (1988), being able to relate and bond with others is one of the most fundamental attributes of humans. There is, however, a downside. "The price we pay for this ability is vulnerability and, eventually, loss. To be open to love, belonging, and intimacy, we must be vulnerable to their absence or their opposites—irrelevance, alienation, isolation, and loss" (Powell 1988, 556).

It is such loss, and the strategies of homeless men to replace those losses, that are the concern of the study. The study's focus included the examination of individuals who adapted to relationship loss, as well as life on the street, by forming street partnerships. Because of the study's focus on both traditional and fictive relationship formation and dissolution, several aspects of the relationships literature will drawn from. By addressing the research on friend and mate selections of the housed population, the roadblocks facing the homeless population will be more easily understood.

The formation of friends is extremely important to individuals as they serve a multitude of functions. Friends provide individuals with a sense of belonging, emotional stability, assistance, physical and emotional support, provide opportunities for communication about him / herself, and a number of other benefits. Relationships are also essential in keeping us physically and mentally healthy. Results from many studies of varying size and methods show that deficiencies in social relationships are associated with increases in physical and mental health problems (i.e., Cohen 1988; House, Umberson, and Landis 1988). Traupmann and Hatfield (1981) concluded that persons who are married, or have close intimates, are generally happier and have less mental and physical illnesses.

Ell (1984) explains that social ties not only increase an individual's well being, they also appear to positively influence people's immunity to physical illnesses and psychological disorders. Ell also contends that social ties aid in a person's ability to solve problems and cope with stress. "Supportive social ties help individuals maintain a balance between environmental demands and personal resources, thereby enhancing host resistance to pathogenic agents such as disease and stress" (Ell 1984, 144).

In attempting to predict psychiatric problems among the homeless population, Calsyn and Morse (1992) suggested that social support did indeed act as a buffer for stress and psychiatric symptoms. For example, both Boa, Whitbeck, and Hoyt (2001) and Unger, Kipke, Simon, Johnson, Montgomery, and Iverson (1998) found that homeless youth who had positive social support networks had lower levels of depression. Still Calsyn and Morse (1992) contend that social support is not enough to remedy the vast array of other problems, such as economic hardship, faced by the homeless.

Given the importance of relationships to our physical and psychological well-being, the process of forming relationships will be addressed in the ensuing section. The relationship literature has yet to dive into the area of same sex partnerships between homeless men. Because of this gap in the literature, it is necessary to turn to the classic research on courtship and friendships in order to ask how, why, and with whom relationships form.

According to Levinger (1983), the physical and social environment, as well as the personalities of the individuals, impacts the possibility of relationship formation. This is not to say that relationship formation is without free choice. Relationships are actively developed and sustained though individual decisions and expectations. However, structure also plays a part in the types and numbers of relationships open to individuals (Allan 1993).

The physical environment inhabited by an individual has a drastic impact on the types and numbers of relationships that may possibly be formed. For example, the size and density of a community, its transportation system, its climate, and a host of other factors all impact with whom an individual may come in contact. In regards to the homeless, whom Snow and Mulcahy (2001) defined as spatially and residentially marginalized, their physical environment and economic backgrounds limited those they could meet. Individuals who are economically stable tend not to frequent homeless shelters, soup kitchens, and campsites under bridges. If the middle and upper class find themselves in these areas, it is either by mistake or because of a work or voluntary commitment. As Levinger points out, "If the physical environment sets the stage, the social environment writes much of the script. Our culture defines rules of eligibility for friendship and mate selection, maps paths over which developing relations are supposed to travel, and writes scenes that help shape relationships at different stages" (1983, 323). A lack of family ties, long-term unemployment or infrequent day labor, and a lack of organizational connections frequently plague the social environments of the homeless and stifle the number and type of relationships available to them.

According to Saegert, Swap, and Zajonc (1973), and the early work of Homans (1961), individuals are also more likely to form relationships with those with whom they come in the most contact. Research on the homeless and impoverished (i.e., McCarthy, Hagan, and Martin 2002; Duneier 1999; Cohen and Sokolovsky 1989) also demonstrate such findings. In examining propinquity's impact on potential relationships, institutional structures and processes as well as individual characteristics must be considered. For example, social variables such as social class, in combination with factors such as de facto segregation, limit the places people may live and work. Individual characteristics like preference for leisure time activities also influence the types of people in which one comes in contact. According to Duck (1991), it is not surprising that individuals typically prefer individuals who share similar attitudes, values, and beliefs. As a consequence of concentrated interactions, people come to share experiences, attitudes, beliefs, and values. In addition, they tend to adopt similar styles of speech and physical appearance (Fischer 1982). Because of these institutional and personal variables, as well as a variety of other factors, there is a general tendency towards homogamy in relationships. A tendency towards homogamy in the relationships formed between homeless men was evident through general observations at the shelter and backed up by the interview data. Homeless men who spent a great deal of time traveling, tramps, tended to associate with fellow tramps rather than home guards that were long-time residents of an area. Associations also developed from common interests such as drugs, alcohol, and employment preference.

Even under the physical and social environments best suited for the formation of relationships, people's personalities and physical characteristics affect their tendencies to form and maintain acquaintanceships (Duck 1977). Moving from the awareness of an individual to a relationship is certainly influenced by whether each person is an introvert, extrovert, aggressive, hot headed, seemingly too busy, physically attractive, and so on (Huston and Levinger 1978). We are also constrained by the information available to us. If the wit of an acquaintance is never revealed, we may lose the chance for a warm friendship (Fischer 1982). In the homeless community, as well as the housed community, there are people who are shy, too aggressive, or physically unkempt, making it difficult for them to form relationships.

The discussion of relationship formation can be directly applied to the lives of the homeless. Homeless individuals are typically transient, even within cities, making the formation of relationships, as described by Homans (1961), difficult. The relative transience of the population, not having set schedules, no home or office at which to meet, social class restraints, physical appearances due to a harsh lifestyle, and meeting places often restricted to crowded public buildings also make the acquisition and maintenance of friendships among the homeless very complex. Such constraints on social ties make even the free choices associated with relationship formation extremely sparse. Despite the very real roadblocks, relationships could be formed and maintained in the homeless community.

Relationships of the Homeless

Disaffiliation. Homeless individuals differ from housed persons in the fact that there is little separation between their public and private spheres. Not being able to retreat to private space is problematic in terms of relationship formation and maintenance. Because the homeless face multiple barriers in establishing and sustaining interpersonal relationships, their situation has often been described as a condition of disengagement from ordinary society.

A great deal of evidence supports the ideas of homeless disaffiliation and extreme isolation (i.e., Lee and Schreck 2005; Lafuente and Lane 1995; Spradley 1970; Bahr 1973; Rossi, Fischer, and Willis 1986). The perspective of disaffiliation assumes that a lack of ties is both a cause and consequence of homelessness. It is assumed that the homeless did not receive adequate support during a time of need and the state of being homeless breaks institutional and network ties. According to Baum and Burnes (1993), disaffiliation is the most universal characteristic of the homeless. In a study by Rossi (1990), less than half of homeless individuals maintained contact with family members, and most had few relationships with other people they could depend on for assistance. Letiecq, Anderson, and Koblinski (1996) examined the social support of homeless and permanently housed low-income mothers with young children. They found that the homeless mothers had significantly less contact with their friends and relatives. They could also count on fewer people for help and childcare during hard times.

Families of Origin. One reason the homeless are typically described as disaffiliated lies in their limited contact with families of origin. While often not totally isolated, the majority of familial relationships available to the homeless in most studies were characterized by infrequent contact and little, if any, exchange of resources. The reasons for limited emotional and economic support from families of origin included, but were not limited to, family separations, institutionalization of children, chemical dependencies, financial instability, family violence, and a reluctance to ask housed family members for assistance. For example, Lee and Schreck (2005) found that almost 30 percent of their sample of homeless individuals had experienced sexual or physical abuse by someone in their home or had been left without adequate food or shelter before turning eighteen. In an examination of the connection between families of origin and homelessness, Reilly (1993) drew out many similar themes from the experiences of those interviewed. The homeless interviewed typically experienced abuse, parental alcoholism, and felt abandoned by their families of origin, whether through adoption, actual abandonment, or gradual loss of contact. Another interesting theme was that many of those interviewed saw themselves as isolated from the communities in which their families lived. This was often a result of a very transient family life which made the establishment of ties very difficult (Reilly 1993). This was especially true of women and children.

According to Brown (1993), studies of homeless women show extremely high rates of physical and sexual assaults. D'Ercole and Struening (1990) interviewed 141 homeless women in New York and found that 63 percent had experienced childhood sexual molestation. In situations like these, persons are not likely to turn to their families for support, and the non-kin they turn to may not be supportive either. Bassuk and Rosenburg (1988) discovered that homeless women had fragmented or nonexistent support networks. They also revealed that homeless women had more contact with victimizing and substance abusing men than women who were housed did. D'Ercole and Struening (1990) also revealed that 60 percent of the homeless women they interviewed had been assaulted by an adult male partner and 58 percent of them had been raped. There is little research in this area on the family experiences of single men.

When studying homeless youth, Tyler, Hoyt, and Whitbeck (2000) and Solarz (1988) found that in addition to physical and sexual abuse, their homes tended to be characterized by high levels of parent-child conflict, discipline problems, and lack of affection. Childhood and adolescent problems in the family often can be connected to an adult life of hardship. Susser et al. (1987) interviewed 918 (223 first-time homeless and 695 longer-term residents of the New York shelter system) homeless men in New York City municipal shelters. Before the age of seventeen, 23 percent of the first-timers and 17 percent of the long-term homeless had been placed in foster care, group homes, or special residences. It was also reported that 43 percent of the first-timers and 34 percent of the long-term shelter residents had exhibited "problem behavior" in their youth, such as running away from home for a week or longer. Problem behavior was defined as being expelled from school or time spent time in a jail or reform school (Susser et al. 1987).

Roman and Wolfe (1995) conducted a study to assess the connection between homelessness and foster care. What they discovered was that there is an overrepresentation (36.2 percent) of people with a foster care history in the United States homeless population. They also revealed that people with a foster care history tend to become homeless at an earlier age when compared to the homeless without such a history (Roman and Wolfe 1995). Piliavin, Sosin, Westerfelt, and Matsueda (1993) examined 331 homeless adults in Minnesota and found that 38.6 percent reported a foster care history, compared to roughly 2 percent in the general population. Piliavin et al. (1993) also found that childhood placement in foster care substantially increased the length of the homeless episode. Similarly, Courtney et al. (2001) interviewed 113 youth who had been emancipated from foster care. Of those interviewed 14 percent of the males and 10 percent of the females stated that they had been homeless at least once since emancipation.

Disaffiliation Challenged. It is such evidence that leads many scholars to conclude that the homeless are truly alienated. Data from this research, as well as a number of studies that will be mentioned in the next section, indicate that a variety of social ties exist within the homeless community, making the description of the homeless as totally isolated misleading. The term disaffiliation is also misleading in that it carried with it assumptions of choice. Blasi (1990) argues that the word disaffiliation implies that homeless individuals disaffiliate and affiliate again when they choose to do so. In reality, some individuals simply do not have access to any social resources because they grew up in institutions or in foster care, or that their families are so impoverished that they can offer no help. "The process here is not one of disaffiliation, but of exhaustion of meager resources, often the inevitable consequence of extreme and persistent poverty" (Blasi 1990, 212).

Despite studies describing homeless who are unable or refuse to rely on the help of friends and housed family members, there are also studies showing considerable assistance from these groups. As argued much earlier by researchers such as Wallace (1965), the types and sources of social support often go unnoticed by outsiders. Data from other studies also directly challenge the ideas that the homeless are suffering from near total isolation (i.e., Dordick 1997; Ruddick 1996; Snow and Anderson 1993; Grisby et al. 1990; Cohen and Sokolovsky 1989; Cohen, Teresi, Holmes, and Roth 1988). One example is the research of Pollio (1994), who followed the residents of an abandoned hotel in Richmond, Virginia. Pollio found that this group formed a community around shared resources, information, and a common identity. In addition to a general community, Pollio (1994) described one street partnership between two homeless men who shared money, food, alcohol and protection. Pollio's description of this single dyad and Dordick's (1997) examination of sexual relations between two homeless men are examples of the few studies to discuss street partnerships.

Although I have been arguing against the universal label of disaffiliation, I concede the fact that being homeless drastically lessens the affiliations of people. Becoming homeless is most often a result of losing not only housing, but support from public institutions, jobs, welfare, and intimate relationships. Thus,

the neighbors, coworkers, professional support, and family that were once at-
tached to a person's social roles are gone, or at least severely strained. The loss
of some affiliations does not directly translate into leading the life of a hermit.
For the homeless it typically translates into social networks that tend to be
smaller and less supportive. These social networks frequently stem from affiliations with those who share similar circumstances, other homeless (Baumann and
Grisby 1988). Grisby et al. (1990) call this process reaffiliation. There is a need
for affiliation that drives people to make friends, join groups, and prefer to do
things with others rather living a solitary existence. The relationships that form
among the homeless are often very important and necessary for survival on the
street. Membership in a network of other homeless people may not only provide
a sense of support and belonging, but also promote psychological well being and
afford a degree of protection from some of the hardships of life on the street
(Grisby et al. 1990).

Sterk-Elifson and Elifson (1992) found that the majority of homeless develop relations with people in similar situations. Although the friendships may
not be incredibly strong, they are often based on qualities of reliability and trust.
In a study of one hundred fifty homeless individuals, La Gory et al. (1991)
found that 79 percent had close friends and that 63 percent received some form
of assistance from friends in the last year. In fact, 60 percent suggested that
friends were helpful when trying to survive on the street. Using a network approach, Mitchell (1987) examined personal support among homeless women and
found that they were indeed able to secure social, emotional, and practical support from those in their same economic predicament. According to La Gory et
al. (1991), as well as results from this study, there is little justification for describing the homeless as totally isolated.

Snow and Anderson (1993) also describe the reliance on friends or acquaintances in similar situations as a survival strategy. They do not paint a picture of friendship groups that rival the functions of the modern family. In fact,
they concede that homeless on homeless crime is drastically higher than rates
that housed individuals inflict on each other. Still, they conclude rates of these
crimes are not as high as one would expect given the harsh living conditions and
scarce resources of the homeless. Snow and Anderson contend that one reason
homeless on homeless crime is less than one would expect is that a "moral code"
governs street life to an extent. The moral code has been described by the saying, "What goes around comes around." This code is practiced in two ways, one
of which inhibits social interaction and another that encourages it. The first way
the code is practiced is through the idea that, "Don't fuck with me and I won't
fuck with you." This is a kind of a truce that keeps many problems from surfac-
ing, but it also keeps strangers as strangers. The way the code serves to bring
individuals together is through a widely acknowledged "norm of reciprocity."
Treating others with a norm or reciprocity "pulls the homeless together, creating
at least a tenuous sense of mutuality and solidarity" (Snow and Anderson 1993,
107-108).

When street friendships are developed, Snow and Anderson (1993) found that they are characterized by quick development but also by superficiality and instability. Although these relationships are often extremely fragile and unstable, they serve important functions. Peer relationships among the homeless provide emotional, material, and informal support that is desperately needed. Limited though it is, social and material support from homeless peers is all too often the only source for street people. According to Snow and Anderson (1993), the necessary, yet fragile relationships between the homeless can be described as quickly formed ties based on modest sharing of resources that are counterbalanced by a chronic distrust of their peers. "These characteristics reflect the impoverished social world of the homeless, a world in which they are largely dislocated from the primary bonds of family and are forecast to live their private lives in caretaker facilities and public places, frequently in the presence of a large number of strangers" (194).

Snow and Anderson contend that life in such places makes the formation and maintenance of friendships difficult, yet a very useful and often necessary survival strategy. In a study of a New York City skid row, the Bowery, Cohen, and Sokolovsky (1989) found numerous examples of the sharing of food, money, and other resources among the residents of the area. Group friendships among homeless and runaway youth were found by McCarthy et al. (2002) and Whitbeck and Hoyt (1999) in which reciprocity was the hallmark of the majority of relationships.

In response to researchers who claim the homeless are on the verge of being an anti-social population, Cohen and Sokolovsky (1989) argue that the living conditions, bottle gangs, community dining, and a host of other activities actually encourage the formation of social groups. Such groups are often times very short lived and far from intimate. According to Cohen and Sokolovsky (1989), buying a bottle of Thunderbird wine for a group of men may entitle you to share in the next bottle, but it does not give you the right to inquire about the names and circumstances of those with whom you are sharing the bottle. Other times these groups are very important in the survival of men on the streets. In a comparison of the social networks of men living in flophouses and those living on the streets of the Bowery, it was discovered that the street networks were smaller (6.0 versus 9.6 linkages) but they were heavily relied upon. The networks of those living on the street were more active in the exchange of necessities such as food, money, and medical assistance (Cohen and Sokolovsky 1989).

As evident in the literature, most researchers stop at the group level when examining the relationships of the homeless. When dyadic relationships are mentioned, they are typically described as a sidebar to a larger study. It is my intention to examine fully the relationships of street partnerships.

Fictive Kin Relationships and the Homeless

Arguing that lifelong road dogs could be seen as fictive kin requires the under-standing that the post-modern family allows for a more fluid definition of kin. Elkind (1994) refers to the postmodern family as the permeable family of the postmodern era because it is open to many forms and is isolated. While the modern family was based on the biological capacity to bear children and the economic interdependence of husband and wife, postmodern relationships are based on personal choice, happiness, and adaptation to structural forces. The recasting of family definitions has allowed for a greater understanding of inti-mate ties between individuals not related by blood or marriage. The most prominent research in this area does not focus on the homeless, but rather on groups that also face issues of economic insecurity. Such studies set the stage for the examination of road dogs as fictive kin.

The first and most studied example of fictive kin relationships can be found in black families. Martin and Martin (1985) describe fictive kinship within the black community as a "caregiving and mutual-aid relationship among non-related blacks that exists because of their common ancestry, history, and social plight" (5). According to Rice (1994), the intergenerational parenting styles of black families are a creative construction of the institution that allows a number of households to exchange social and economic resources. More specific to friendship networks, Taylor and Chatters (1986) found that elderly black men in their study received more support, particularly socioemotional support, from their friends than from relatives.

In one of the most influential examinations of the topic, Stack (1974) also found the creation of kin networks among non-related poor African American communities. Within the black community studied by Stack, black men and women drew on the resources of fictive kin to meet the roadblocks to daily liv-ing. Exchanges of services and goods were a prime strategy in living on limited incomes. These kin groups practiced resource sharing, called "swapping," which was a tool helpful in daily survival. According to Stack, the bond of kin is hon-ored through shared history and common worldviews. The persons seen as fic-tive kin were honored with the same deference and respect given to blood rela-tives. The ties and obligations to the family were also as strong as those with blood relatives (Stack 1974).

In a rare deviation from ethnographic data in this area, Chatters, Taylor, and Jayakody (1994) used a national sample of black adults to examine the predomi-nance of fictive kin. Describing fictive kin as persons who were not related by blood or marriage, but were treated like relatives, they found two-thirds of the sample indicated at least one such member of their family.

Liebow's (1967) work can be presented as support for the existence of fic-tive kin relationships in both the homeless and black communities. The relation-ships described by Liebow typically formed between coworkers and other area residents who spent considerable time on the streets. On Tally's corner, black men and women referred to some peers as quasi-siblings. The terms "going for brothers" or "going for sisters" was used to describe when two men or women present themselves as brothers/sisters to the outside world. Liebow (1967) does mention one man and woman "going for cousins" in a non-sexual friendship, but cross sex fictive relationships among similar aged individuals appeared to be quite rare. These fictive kin relationships were not only social ties, but valuable resources for individuals who were short of money (Liebow 1967).

In addition to the work being done on African American kin networks, fictive relationships have been found in new immigrant communities, in prison populations, among the elderly, and same sex partnerships. Ebaugh and Curry (2000) found fictive kin systems in new immigrant communities to be important sources of social and economic capital. Large kin systems were also found in correctional facilities. According to Pollock-Byrne (1990), pseudo families can be found in female, male, and juvenile correctional facilities. When comparing the incidence of pseudo families in male and female prisons, however, the female rates appear to be much higher. Fictive kin relationships have also been documented in less expansive networks. For example, Mac Rae (1992) conducted interviews with 142 elderly women and found that 40 percent could identify a fictive family member, described as meaningful and salient components of their social networks. Karner (1998) described fictive kin ties between elderly and homecare workers as giving the elderly a sense of the cultural ideal of family caregiving and the ability to seek, and receive, assistance on tasks that are not the assigned duties of the employee.

Most of the work on fictive kinship deals with populations in dire economic circumstances. Weston's work diverged from this theme and conducted an in-depth study of gay and lesbian friendship networks and families in the San Francisco Bay area who were not dependent on fictive relationships for survival. Weston (1997), while disagreeing with the label "fictive," described the progression into a family as a process in which relationships based on companionship developed into intimate ties where the members think and refer to each other as family. According to Weston, these groups engage in emotional bonding and material assistance which gives rise to a sense of belonging which makes these groups as much a family as heterosexual couples.

Although the black family, prison inmates, recent immigrants, the elderly, and gay and lesbian families often dwell in entirely different social and economic circumstances, their adaptations of "typical" family life may not be entirely different from those of the homeless. Whether for social or economic reasons, many individuals cannot, or choose not, to follow traditional norms when creating family. In the same way that black, elderly, inmates, and same-sex families must be resourceful in creating friendship and fictive kin relationships, the homeless often establish fictive kin relationships outside blood relations. These studies provide a foundation from which to discuss relationships between homeless men as fictive kin relationships.

According to Wagner (1993), many of the homeless people he interviewed adapted to life on the street not by returning to their families of origin or by forming their own nuclear family. Instead, they established friendship communities, engaged in serial relationships, or formed partnerships. These adaptations were often made because families of origin and creation could not always be counted on. In describing the adaptations of family life, Wagner (1993) found a considerable amount of mutual aid among non-related people. For example, Wagner identified fictive "mothers of the street" who frequently assisted the homeless in gaining shelter. Among what Wagner (1993) called street drunks, the term "cousin" was used to describe relationships between fictive kin.

Rivlin and Imbimbo (1989) examined a squatter community in New York City. They found that a strong community was established around the idea and framework of a family. The group centered around two founders of the community, the "mother" and the "father." These two established rules, acted as spokespersons to the media when reporters visited the community, and directed activities such as group cooking and the acquisition of food. According to Rivlin and Imbimbo (1989), a "family-like social pressure" existed that helped maintain order and the following of rules. This pseudo family not only created family rules, but also rallied around those in the community who needed extra attention and support in times of illness or other hardships. Wright and Draus (1997) conducted participant observations and interviewed homeless African American men living in Chicago. They discovered that among the men who made their homes on concrete landings beneath a major street, families often emerged out of the continued contact and the sharing of limited resources. As reported by Wright and Draus (1997), the formation of street families was not spontaneous. Instead, they were a deliberate creation of a family and must be understood in the context of the disintegration of their safety net. In a study of single-room-occupancy tenements, Siegal (1978) credits the formation of "quasi-familial arrangements" for the survival of many of the alcoholic male residents.

In a study of homeless youth, McCarthy et al. (2002) distinguished between groups of street friends and fictive street families. Street friends and street families differed in that families spent more time together, relied more on each other for social and economic support, and were more likely to develop feelings of trust, commitment, and solidarity. Membership in street families reduced criminal victimization by providing information about how to be safe on the street, and fictive kin could also be counted on for protection when necessary.

Dordick's (1997) study of four homeless groups in New York City demonstrated how street relationships are often situational. The four groups resided in a train station, a squatter's camp called the shanty, a small private shelter, and the armory, a large city-owned shelter of last resort. In the small private shelter where the few morning and evening hours spent at the shelter were consumed with cleaning up after meals and preparing for bed, few relationships were formed. In the shanty, a small squatter camp, sexual relationships were formed between opposite sex partners. In two sites, the armory and the station, Dordick identified groups of homeless men who spent considerable time together, shared resources, and identified each other as associates. Due to the danger of living on the streets near the station and the danger of living in the armory, what Dordick described as a shelter plagued by violence and a lack of control by staff, group affiliation provided the protection many men needed.

A second type of relationship, one fitting of the fictive label, was also identified at the armory. These male dyadic partnerships were on many levels similar to the road dogs found in The Living Room. These relationships involved partnerships based on exchanges of resources that ultimately became more family-like. Both Dordick's group and those found in Plainview offered each other emotional support, exchange of resources, and protection. Family terminology was also used to describe many such relationships, but the terms used differed in one important capacity. Dordick's partnerships were called "marriages" and often involved sexual relationships. These marriages were described by one of the participants in Dordick's study as similar to sexual relationships found in prison, in that men were involved in activities they may not participate in when living under different circumstances. Dordick expanded such descriptions and noted that relationships could be formed between two straight men, a straight man and a homosexual "wife," or a "MO" (transgendered) and a straight man. When non-sexual relationships were formed between two straight males, they were often assumed to be sexually involved by other homeless men if they appeared to be close.

These marriages, as with road dogs, began out of necessity and were exchange-based. Because shelter residents could not count on their shelter to consistently provide them with protection or food, they sought the provisions of such necessities through the help of other residents. According to Dordick, "marriages are a solution to the problems inherent in needing to rely on others in a violent and impoverished environment" (1997, 147). In describing these marriages, the process of relationship formation and shift from economic support to emotional attachments, where unbalanced exchanges were accepted, was similar to lifelong road dogs that were found it the study of Plainview's homeless. However, there is nothing in the interview data of the thirty-three road dog informants which suggests that any of their fictive relationships were sexual.

Conclusion

When a person becomes homeless, it is typically because they have exhausted all their potential resources. While many homeless do not seek alternative sources of aid, many others deal with the lack of resources by partnering up with another homeless individual. Distinguishing between those who establish relationships with other homeless, road dogs, and those who do not, loners, is the crux of this study.

Fictive kin relationships, like other intimate ties, are not of one framework or model. Still, what they do as a whole is to demonstrate the inability of the traditional monolithic family model to serve as our one definition of family. Economic and survival issues bring the partners together, but on occasion they become interdependent and develop relationships that fulfill functions typically undertaken by family members. In this study, these partnerships were sought out in order to explore their utility and the appropriateness of the term fictive kin. Additionally, homeless loners were included as a comparison group for the assessment of relationships with families of origin, created families, and fictive kin. Not only is research lacking on road dogs, but ties to families of origin have received little attention and research on created kin is sparse. The lack of research on these subjects, as well as the timely question of what actually constitutes a family, makes it clear that this is a fertile area for research.

Chapter Three

Road Dogs and Loners

There are many ways to categorize the homeless. Men on the street could be classified by length of time without a home, their veteran status, whether or not they suffered from addictions, or a host of other characteristics. This study's focus on relationships called for a different approach. Given that the main focus centered on the reasons for and extent to which homeless men utilized personal relationships, comparing road dogs and loners became an obvious choice. This study examined the connections of both road dogs and loners to housed family members and other homeless men. Although loners and road dogs frequented the same shelter, waited for day labor on the same corner, and had many of the same experiences with the law and military, their experiences were far from identical.

Loners

People who tend to experience life in relative solitude, often referred to as loners, can be found in all social classes. While loners are described in many studies, in-depth examinations of loners and comparisons to other sub-categories of homeless men are quite rare in homeless research. Kipke, Unger, O'Connor, Palmer, and LeFrance's (1997) study of over seven hundred fifty homeless and runaway youth is a noted exception. In their study, 12 percent of the sample identified as loners. When compared to four other subgroups of homeless youth (punks/skinheads, druggies, hustlers, and gang members), loners were more likely to receive government entitled benefits and less likely to draw support from family members. In the current study, informants who referred to themselves as loners also were less likely to rely on family members for support. In terms of not seeking support from their peers, informants typically offered three general reasons for not partnering up. These reasons include not being able to trust fellow homeless persons, not wanting to be hassled by the needs of someone else, and issues of mental health.

Issues of Trust and Nuisance

Trust was a major theme running throughout the entire study. Trust was used to describe why partnerships were formed, why they failed, or why they were never attempted. Sandy, now thirty-one years old, began running away at age thirteen. He explained his level of trust toward his homeless counterparts. "You can't depend on street people. They will stab you in the back. They can talk all that friendship and everything, but on the streets they will turn their back on you. So I am pretty much a loner."

Road dogs typically cited partnering up as a way to make life easier, but many loners argued the opposite. To loners, having to deal with the needs and actions of a traveling partner was simply a nuisance. In the interviews, loners were more likely to express that they did not need help from anyone and that they preferred that way of life. Kurt, a forty-three-year-old loner who has not seen his family in years, represents the theme of not wanting to be dependent on or responsible for another person. As Kurt explained, "I'm more of a loner and I like to live my own life. I don't like to be dependent on anybody. I like to depend on myself. I like to try to take care of myself and my own shit. That's just the way I am. That's the way I was brought up and raised." He went on to say:

> My stepfather is deceased and my father is still alive but we don't have anything to do with one another. I've got two stepsisters and we don't have anything to do with one another. Like I said, I'm more or less a loner. I'm not one to ask people for very much so I choose not to be around them and if I'm out here, I'm not around them. I don't have to ask them for anything.

When asked why he did not travel with a road dog, Marten, a thirty-one-year-old eighth-grade drop-out, responded:

> It is just a hassle. If you are on a train, you don't have to worry about getting caught because the other guy is looking around and walking around. You don't have to babysit or worry about them. It is just yourself. As far as settling down in a town, you don't have to worry about supporting him or if he is going to steal. You know what I mean? It is just easier that way.

I'm Just a Loner

A more general, though extremely complicated, reason was also consistently offered. Related to issues of mental health, many informants stated that they did not partner up because they were "more or less a loner." Being in a depressed state can impede an individual's ability to reciprocate emotionally or materially with others, thus becoming alienated from those who could provide support (Keefe and Roberts 1984). While this study did not test for psychological problems in informants, several studies have concluded that social isolation and loneliness are a pervasive problem among the homeless (i.e., Rokach 2005; Rokach 2004; Fisk and Frey 2002). When 266 homeless individuals were compared with 595 housed men and women, Rokach (2005) discovered that homeless individuals were more likely to be lonely and also to experience their loneliness differently than the general population. For example, the homeless scored higher on measures of interpersonal isolation and self-alienation than the general population. In a study of "shopping-bag-ladies," Coston (1989) revealed that of the study participants who reported extreme loneliness, one-fourth expressed a desire to have greater contact with the rest of society but did not for two reasons. The homeless feared victimization and also believed that people never took the time to acknowledge their presence. In attempt to measure the physical and mental health of Plainview's homeless population, county officials estimated that 38 percent suffered from mental health problems (Urban Development Department 1996).

In addition to loneliness and isolation, schizophrenia (Kelly 2005) and other mental disorders (Fischer and Breakey 1991) have been found in significantly higher levels among the homeless. For example, Lloyd-Cobb and Dixon (1995) cited higher rates of depression and anxiety, likely linked to the stress of not being able to easily secure basic human needs. Recent studies on homeless and runaway youth could lead to a better understanding of homeless adults who identify as loners. For example, Tyler, Cauce, and Whitbeck (2004) contend that neglect, physical abuse, and sexual abuse that many homeless and runaway youth are exposed to may lead to dissociative behaviors, ultimately impacting their mental health.

Arguably, the presence of psychological problems is higher among the homeless, but that was not the focus of this research. Because psychological classification of informants was not the intent of the study, self-classifications of individuals as loners or road dogs were taken at face value. For example, Danny, thirty-five years old, was in the middle of a legal battle to secure visitation with his six-year-old son. Although he moved to Plainview's streets from Kansas to be near his son, his visits had been few and far between. Danny gave a detailed explanation of his situation when asked why he has quit all the jobs he has ever had:

> They diagnosed me as having an anti-social personality with schizoid features. You know what that is, a loner. I am a natural born loner. I just have a hell of a time getting around people, relating to people. I always have. I started drinking a lot back then and it's been a problem ever since. I have a hangover right now. I walked about six miles today trying to walk it off. I tried a couple of pitchers last night with one of my Hispanic friends. I knew I shouldn't have done it. It is not the work (Talking about why he eventually quits all his jobs). It is the enormous strain of being forced to deal with people. It's such a burden for me that living this way is actually easier for me. Most people can't understand it. They say, "Why do you do that to yourself?" I say, "Well, the alternative is working or stealing and I am not a thief." It (homelessness) is just easier.

Kurt, also a loner, spent a few brief periods with road dogs, but explained to me what happened when the men began to get close:

> I've had friends of mine that I've met on the road that I've been with for six months or a year. And those people, some of them you become roommates with and some of them you become very close to. You get more intimate, more on a personal basis. Not intimate like in a love relationship, but intimate as a stronger friendship. And that's where the problem comes in. It's not really a problem, but it's a problem for me because I don't have any family and I really don't want any. I'm a loner like I said and that's basically the way I want to stay. I want to keep my space.

Kurt's comments demonstrate why the line between road dogs and loners cannot always be clearly drawn. A small number of loners took traveling partners out of what they described as necessity but they rarely lasted more that a few days. Kurt was the only self-defined loner to mention taking a road dog for any length of time. Most loners in the study did have acquaintances and found some level of support from the larger homeless community but other than rare situations, they only sought shelter or traveled alone. The confidence of the loners as to their reasons for limiting their contact with other homeless individuals was certainly a strong theme throughout the research. Just as strong, however, was the confidence from road dogs that partnering up was a better strategy for living on the streets.

Road Dogs

I first heard the term road dog used in an interview with Chris, a forty-two-year-old former oil field laborer from Louisiana. Chris lost interest in school and eventually dropped out after his father's death on an offshore oil rig. When Chris turned eighteen, he followed in his father's footsteps and went to work offshore. He remained offshore for around twenty years, but lost his job when the oil market turned sour in the early 1990s. Since then, Chris has traveled across the United States working as a trucker, a roofer, in a meatpacking plant, and as a day laborer. His lack of a high school education and the corresponding inability to secure steady employment resulted in numerous stints of homelessness. While working as a day laborer and living in a Minnesota homeless shelter, Chris teamed up with Marty, his most recent road dog. I met Chris and Marty as they were riding three-speed bicycles from northern Minnesota to the Louisiana coast. Their ultimate goal is to find work with the oil companies.

Trust

Unlike loners, road dogs are by definition partners. This is not to say that homeless men who are willing to partner up do so constantly or indiscriminately. Many tend to travel alone for the same reasons mentioned by loners, lack of trust and not wanting to bother, but will partner up when they meet the right person. Meeting the right person ultimately boiled down to finding someone they could trust. Real trust, however, did not always develop until the relationship had a chance to grow. Marty explained how his level of trust with Chris, his road dog, had grown over the first few hundred miles of their trip:

> It's kind of like we're one person but we're able to actually be in two places at one time. We don't pay attention to who has more money. If I run out of cigarettes, he buys them for me. If I am in a store and he wants a pop, I'll grab him a pop. And that is where the dependability starts to fall into place and you start to have a level of trust. When you are flying twenty miles an hour down a hill and he yells "car," I take his word for it. It's the little things that start to add up on a daily basis. Soon you go, "Ok, this is somebody that I can trust. I can believe what he tells me." If I were to tell him something in confidence, I would feel that it would be kept without reservation. He is kind of like an adopted family. I depend on him more than I depend on my family. It is just one of those things. It is really hard to explain.

Companionship

While finding someone you can trust is a necessity in forming a partnership, there must be a reason for two men to even consider partnering up. Theme analysis revealed that homeless men who partnered up typically did so because they were seeking companionship, they found someone with whom they shared a common goal, or they were simply trying to survive. Ricky, a thirty-three-year-old drug-addicted road dog, became homeless after his house burnt down. He offered his main reason for partnering up:

> One reason people travel together is companionship. It gets lonely. I don't want to be alone. Wallowing in your own pile of poop can get pretty down and miserable. But if you have got somebody else with you, that seems not to happen as much. Someone can drive themselves crazy being alone.

More simply stated by Stan, a thirty-seven-year-old home guard who grew up on the same block The Living Room is located, "You look less homeless when you sit in a restaurant drinking coffee for hours if you are with somebody." Stan is practicing what Goffman (1963) referred to a stigma management. When people have a stigmatizing attribute, in this case homelessness, controlling information about your stigma is the best way to reduce the "spoiling" of their identity. By managing his impression by appearing to be catching up with a friend rather than simply trying to stay warm and passing the time, he disguised his potentially discrediting attribute (Goffman 1963). On a practical level, this afforded him more time in a warm place and more refills of his coffee.

Common Goals

The second theme revealed through analysis of the interview data was that sharing a common goal was essential to partnership formation. In the words of Trevor, a fifty-two-year-old road dog who appeared to be in his late sixties, "When you partner up with somebody, it's usually somebody in the same situation or who's got the same deal going on you have." In addition to simple companionships the shared interests found among informants typically included finding work, the desire to travel, and the consumption of drugs and alcohol.

Finding Work. Most men in the study, including those with road dogs, tended to seek work alone. However, there were those who did so as a pair. This typically involved sporadic employment through day labor and did not entail only taking jobs as a team, but the understanding that both partners were seeking work and the day's pay would be shared. The advantage of seeking work in pairs resembled an insurance policy. When one person was not able to find work on any given day, they had a backup income supply from their partner's efforts. The general rule was whoever had money paid for the evening's needs such as food, cigarettes, alcohol, etc. These items were shared rather than borrowed. The majority of road dogs claim they did not keep a mental checklist of which person bought the last pack of cigarettes or hamburger. Instead, it was all believed to even out in the long run.

Less traditional ways to seek employment were also revealed by the informants. They included "flying a sign" or using your "credit card" ("will work for food" signs), selling plasma, and a multitude of illegal acts. Mark, whose street name is Mexican Mark, was a forty-four-year-old who came from an abusive home in which his father murdered his mother. For a year and a half, he traveled with his road dog stealing from stores and then returning the merchandise for cash. Mark, however, did not consider what he does stealing. In fact, he refused to partner up with thieves (those who do not return the stolen goods). It should be noted that most of the informants made it clear that anything other than trying to secure legitimate work, such as seeking day labor, was looked down upon. Mark's tactics were not the norm among the informants and even panhandling was seen by most informants as giving "real homeless" a bad name.

Alcohol and Drugs. Securing drugs and alcohol also brought partners together. The Plainview Health Department estimated that approximately one-fourth of the homeless population in Plainview had a substance abuse problem (Urban Development Department 1996). Snow and Anderson (1993) described "circling up" where men would pool money to buy alcohol for the evening. Contributing was not a necessary requirement for consumption because the principle of "what goes around comes around" served as the insurance for future contribution. The following observation came from Jason, a thirty-nine year-old loner who did not drink because alcoholism was a severe problem in his family. Even though he is a loner, he was able to offer some insight as to one reason road dogs partnered up. He described the partnerships that formed on the street around the consumption of alcohol: "Some of the buddy-types drink. It is like a drinking buddy type thing, you know. If one doesn't have it, they rely on the other person for it. If one has got the money, they go get a twelve pack. The next day the other might have the money. They rely on that so it's somewhat of a bonding thing." Not only was the code of the streets reflected in these relationships, but also social exchange theory, which will be used to analyze the relationships of road dogs more thoroughly in Chapter 7.

Partnerships and groups also formed around the acquisition and use of illegal drugs. In addition to stories of personal addictions and hardships, many road dogs talked about the social aspects of drug use. Troy is a thirty-seven-year-old road dog from Plainview who began running away from home after his father was sent to prison for raping Troy's sister. He detailed his first two years on the street:

> That is what I would do with my time, my free time. I would party with who- ever it was that happened to be handy that I would find on the streets. That was my first exposure to street life. Like I said, I probably spent a year and a half or two living among the street people. Not necessarily living under bridges be- cause there was always the party crowd. Someone would always lend you a couch or a floor to sleep on. I did live in burnt-out or abandoned homes several times just because that particular day nobody came along and said, "I have a place for you to sleep."

The groups Troy discussed were not intimate dyads, but rather fluid groups. Most party groups, or bottle gangs, sprung up quickly and dispersed when the common interest had been consumed. While the larger groups tended to be fluid and include many strangers, they often had a core membership in which a few of the men became quite close and dependent on each other. From these interac- tions road dog relationships were often formed. Road dogs repeatedly discussed meeting men in these groups that shared common interests. If common interests were found in someone that could be trusted, partnerships sometimes developed.

One of the most interesting findings was a different pattern of drug use among loners and road dogs. In the case of alcohol, both loners and road dogs had high levels of use and abuse and would find partners, groups, or even strangers to share a bottle. Drugs appear to be a different case. While ten of the thirty-three road dogs mentioned serious issues involving drugs, not one loner mentioned the use of illegal drugs. It is possible that because drugs were harder to procure and were more expensive than alcohol, it took more of a group effort to obtain them. Cocaine and marijuana were the most frequently mentioned drugs. It is possible that the tendency for it to be a group activity, along with issues of trust, and dangers involved with taking drugs when you are alone on the street, discouraged loners in the study from engaging in drug use anywhere near the levels of men who were willing to partner up. It is also possible that informants' need for drugs drove them to group membership, thus ultimately categorizing themselves as someone who was willing to partner up. Given the difficulty in addressing the different patterns of drug use among loners and road dogs in this study, a more extensive examination of this phenomenon is certainly warranted.

Partnering up based on common issues of substance use did not always mean consumption was the goal. While in Boston, Ricky partnered up with another drug addict who was also trying to remain clean. Ricky and his road dog were living in a shelter and on a waiting list for a drug and alcohol treatment program. Ricky explained how partners could be used to both help refrain from and obtain drugs and alcohol:

> I partnered up with somebody else trying to get into the program and get some help with his addiction. We kept each other strong. We kept each other out of drug streets, liquor stores, and stuff like that. And when you are not in that frame of mind (trying to stay sober), you just want to be drunk or whatever. So you partner up with somebody that's going to be willing to work to get drinking money or whatever.

Travel. The final common goal among the road dogs in the study was the desire, or need, to travel. Many men, especially tramps, mentioned that they could only stay stationary for a limited amount of time before they would yield to the urge to hit the rails or the road. Snow and Anderson (1993) described traditional tramps as having a hobo type life-style that included a pattern of working, drinking, and traveling. Many times these partnerships started much more quickly than partnerships based on other goals and needs. The quick development of these road dog relationships was emphasized through the experiences of Chuck, a thirty-nine-year-old self-defined tramp.

> I partnered up with Lobo for about six months. It was kind of funny. I was on a rail coming out of Southern California and he jumped the same car I was on. I usually don't like to ride the same car with another guy. It is just one of the rules of the rail. But we hit it off and we talked and got along so we decided to run for awhile together. We just ran across the U.S.A.

In part due to quick development, traveling partnerships tend to last only until the desired destination changes. Chuck's six-month partnership with his road dog, Lobo, was actually much longer than most relationships that start in similar ways.

Survival

The most frequently cited reason that informants offered for partnering up was survival. Homelessness is not an easy life. Being homeless frequently means wondering where your next meal will come from, where you will sleep, where you can get a drink, and where you can hang out to avoid hassles from the police. With all of these and many more daily concerns, friendships and partnerships were found to be useful and often necessary tools for survival.

Partnerships initiated with the goal of making street life more bearable generally centered on the exchange of resources or services. When individuals would pool their money and muscle, survival became a bit easier. In fact, having someone to turn to for support or protection was described by most road dogs as a necessity. Ricky offered a general explanation of why partnerships were important:

> In my way of looking at it, it is almost a must. If you are a loner and you got your camp somewhere, you never know what is going to happen to you. If you're out at night people come up and beat the shit out of you. They beat you up and try to see if you have any money. If you've been drinking too much and pass out somewhere and you ain't got a buddy with you, you're always in danger. With the homeless people there are good and there are bad. We share and look out for each other but there are some of those people that are just out for themselves and try and take advantage of people. And that's the main reason why I always have somebody. Also, it is a lot easier to for two people to get ahead or try to get themselves out of a situation like that. You know two heads are better than one a lot of the times. Getting money together to be able to rent a hotel room for a week or something. You know you pay $180 a week getting a hotel room. It's hard by yourself, but if you get two people, you just split it in half. It gets done a lot easier.

As Ricky demonstrated, the streets can be dangerous. The often cited code of the streets is an ideal with the reality of street life being somewhat different. While informants constantly referred to cases where other homeless, often strangers, offered assistance to them, they were also cautious about whom they trusted. Many homeless the informants came in contact with simply did not live by the codes of reciprocity and "what goes around comes around."

Nels, who had lived in Plainview ten years earlier, found himself back in town just prior to the interview. He had been tramping (traveling) for the majority of the past decade. When asked to describe people on the street, he described the homeless as "beautiful people" whom he could ask for a cigarette or change to get a cup of coffee. Any homeless person would give it to him, he claimed, because he would do the same for them. After describing the beautiful people, he went on to say that there were also the ones that were not so nice. They were the ones that you have to look out for because they were out to steal your things and could turn on you at any time. According to Nels, they were simply people you had to learn to deal with. Danny, a loner, also expressed caution when dealing with fellow homeless. "A lot of street people have a lot of character defects, you know, they can't be trusted. I'd say that deep down most street people probably dislike each other. They know that they'll see each other off and on around places like this so we force ourselves to be cordial or affable with the others. Most of them I don't like at all. I talk to them, joke around with them, but I don't like them."

In describing his time living on the streets of Kansas City, Don described how partners were needed for safety. Don, forty-two years old, spent most of the last twenty years living on the street, in missions, and Salvation Army programs. Don's interview took place in the very first apartment he had rented independently in his life. At the time of the interview, Don had been in his apartment and off the streets for two days. Reflecting on the times he spent on the streets in his hometown, Don described Kansas City as "a gang town" that possessed many dangers to the homeless. Don's claims of street dangers are backed up by a number of studies examining homeless victimization (i.e., Lee and Schreck 2005; Burt, Aron, Lee, and Valente 2001; Wenzel, Koegel, and Gelberg 2000; Snow, Baker, and Anderson 1989). Because many homeless find the practice of missions locking in residents early in the evening stifling, many homeless prefer to camp out in nicer weather despite the risks. Don believes that it is safer when you are with a partner or a group because, "If you are walking around and you have a bedroll and a back pack, you are marked."

Later in the interview, Don described the usefulness of partners in a less dangerous situation. Don discussed how he would commonly hit dumpsters with his road dog. In one instance Don and his partner discovered one hundred pounds of cheese in the dumpster of a Safeway grocery store. Because there was more cheese than they could possibly eat, they took it to a city park and gave it away to other tramps. The fact that Don and his partner shared with other tramps demonstrates how survival on the streets is not aided only through partners. When asking about informal support available to people walking into The Living Room for the first time, Craig, a drug-addicted alcoholic with monumental health problems, described a recent scenario. According to Craig, a few weeks earlier a couple of guys had just jumped off the train from Colorado and were inquiring about places they could get some warm clothes. Beyond telling them where they could get free clothing, Craig gave them each two bus passes that he had been saving so they could get to the Good Neighbor house for clothing and back to The Living Room for lunch. In detailing his actions, Craig stated that he tries to be as helpful as he can and that he treats all people with respect as long as they treat him the same.

It appears that friends, partners, and even strangers in a similar situation could be very useful on the street. Strangers offer advice and transportation and partners watch each other's backs and dumpster-dive together. Loners have demonstrated that life on the street is possible without taking a partner, but according to road dogs, the rules of survival are clear: two are better than one.

Different Traits and Experiences

The basic differences between road dogs and loners translated into a host of distinct traits and experiences. First and foremost, they differed in their level of affiliation. Affiliation was measured by a twenty-six item scale constructed by La Gory et al. (1991). The demographic comparisons were based on the entire sample but the affiliation scale was completed by the thirty-five most recently interviewed informants (twenty-five road dogs and ten loners).

In order to address the issue of affiliation, La Gory et al. (1991) utilized a survey designed to assess instrumental support from friends and relatives as measured by the receipt of money, food, clothing, shelter, rides, advice, and healthcare as well as contact with relatives in the two months prior to the interview. They conducted a quota sample of one hundred fifty homeless men in Birmingham, Alabama and concluded their sample was not isolated. In combining the four sub-scales for a more comprehensive measure of affiliation, a mean level of 10.58 (*sd* = 5.73) was reported for their sample.

In order to triangulate the interview data, the affiliation scale was utilized in the current study. While this study did not include a matched sample of housed informants, the results suggest that the sample was, as with the Birmingham study, not completely isolated. The mean level of affiliation for the thirty-five informants was 12.8 (*sd* = 5.54). All items were dummy coded, making the possible range 0 to 26. The sample's range was two to twenty-four.

Results from the affiliation scale and three of the four subscales consistently show higher rates of affiliation among road dogs. The mean level of affiliation for loners was 8.90 (*sd* = 4.01) compared to 14.36 (*sd* = 5.53) for road dogs. An examination of the range also helps to demonstrate the groups' differences. For loners the range was two to fifteen compared to road dog's affiliation range of five to twenty-four.

The twenty-six item scale can also be broken down into four sub-scales. The first subscale, a six item measure of expressive ties, had the lowest level of reliability (Cronbach's Alpha = .263) and the smallest difference between the two groups. The six questions include measures of contact with relatives and friends as well as their overall assessment of how many people they could count on. The mean level of affiliation in the expressive subscale among loners was 2.89 (*sd* = 1.83) compared to 2.91 (*sd* = 1.12) for road dogs. Examination of individual questions within the expressive subscale also helped provide a description of the presence of ties among the sample. Because only thirty-five surveys were collected, results from individual questions will be addressed only in general terms. Approximately two-thirds of all informants did not visit, talk to, or write their parents at least once every two or three months. Over two-thirds did not contact any relatives every two or three months. In contrast, over three-fourths claimed to have a close friend in Plainview they could ask for advice or help. Informants were also asked, "On the whole do you feel that you have enough people to turn to, or would you be happier if you had more to turn to?" Almost two-thirds of all informants stated they "had enough" people they could turn to. Despite the higher overall level of affiliation among road dogs, and the similarity of expressive ties, three-fourth of loners stated they had enough people to turn to, compared to just over half of road dogs. Although this is a very interesting finding, it should be interpreted cautiously. It is possible that the results are tainted by the difficulty of the question or as a way to reduce cognitive dissonance. It is hard for someone to admit that they do not have enough people to which to turn. An indication that this may be the case is revealed in the fact that three informants stated that they could not answer this question. It is also quite possible that the results were not at all tainted and loners answered the question in an informed manner. As a loner, it is likely that they felt they had enough to people to turn to because they were not comfortable turning to anyone for help.

The results from the expressive subscale did not demonstrate large differences between the groups, but the following subscales paint a different picture. Two seven-item subscales measure instrumental support from both relatives and friends. Informants were asked if they had received money, advice, food, clothing, a place to stay, a ride, or healthcare from each group in the year prior to the interview. Mean levels of support from relatives (Cronbach's Alpha = .892) were found to be 1.30 (sd = 2.36) for loners and 2.76 (sd = 2.57) for road dogs. Instrumental support from friends (Cronbach's Alpha = .901) was measured as means of 3.40 (sd = 2.95) and 5.08 (sd = 2.31) for loners and road dogs respectively.

The final subscale (Cronbach's Alpha = .840) included six items assessing the presence of named acquaintances during six periods of the day (breakfast, after breakfast, lunch, after lunch, dinner and after dinner). Informants were given a "1" if they named a person they "usually have breakfast with" and a "0" if they consistently spent that time alone. The mean level of acquaintances among loners was 1.20 (sd = 1.48) compared to 3.52 (sd = 2.12) for road dogs.

Examination of demographic data, available for all forty-five informants, was also useful in analyzing the common themes and experiences of the informants. Affiliation was also measured by looking at the marital and child rearing experiences of the men. Only three of the informants were currently married and two of those three had not seen their wives in years. Just over one-third of the informants, the majority being road dogs, were divorced or widowers. Almost 60 percent of the informants, just over one-half of the road dogs and two-thirds of the loners, had never been married. Forty-four percent of the sample had no children. Of the informants with children, road dogs were more likely to be parents than were loners.

The affiliation scale and the demographic data supported the interview data by providing a tool for making direct comparisons between road dogs and loners. With the exception of the expressive sub-scale, road dogs did appear to have had more contact and exchange greater levels of support with friends and relatives. While these distinctions could be found, it would be premature to conclude that the practice of partnering-up or remaining more isolated created two completely distinct realities on the street. In providing a clearer picture of the survival strategies and relationship structures of homeless men, the shared traits and experiences of road dogs and loners need to be examined.

Shared Traits and Experiences

Despite the important distinction that road dogs appeared to be afforded more support on the street, road dogs and loners share many similar characteristics, experiences, and tales of hardship. According to the director of The Living Room, there may not be an average client, but a variety of common themes could be found in their lives.

> The common things are lack of education, lack of social skills, and some level of repeated failures. A lot of these folks have been battered since childhood. Whether they were raised in an alcoholic family or their family wasn't very supporting or very loving. Maybe it was abusive. For most of our folks their acceptance of the American dream is less. "I am not going to get the BMW and the big house and blah, blah, blah." Their dream is just getting by and surviving. I think a lot of them probably constantly deal with issues of depression and issues of drugs, alcohol, and mental health. The report is that 60 to 65 percent have some issue of mental health or drug and alcohol problems. The other group, that 30 or so percent, after being on the street for a long enough period of time, start to develop issues of alcohol and issues of mental health because it is a burden. It is a constant battle to be on the street. Every day it is "where am I sleeping, where am I getting my food, where am I going to get my dental, where am I going to a doctor or get a prescription filled." Every day is a day of stress. The thought is, "they are healthy, why not go out and get a job?" These people have been trained generation after generation after generation to not have the skills to go out there and get jobs.

The common themes mentioned by the current director also surfaced through the analysis of the interviews. In addition to patterns of alcohol and drug use that were previously discussed, education, military service, troubles with the law, health concerns, and patterns of work came to light in the interviews.

Education

In terms of educational attainment, no contrasting patterns emerged between road dogs and loners. The overall level of education was not very high among the sample. The mean for the number of years spent in school was 11.56 (*sd* = 2.3). Fourteen informants did not finish high school (31.1 percent), twenty-two graduated from high school or obtained their GED (48.9 percent), six had attended college (13.3 percent) and three had a college degree (6.7 percent). These findings are similar to national-level data that estimated approximately 37 percent of homeless individuals having obtained less than a high school graduation or equivalent and 27 percent having at least some college credit (Burt et al. 1999).

Of the informants who did not graduate from high school several patterns emerged as to why they dropped out. The reasons consistently offered by informants included being a bad student, associations with the wrong crowd, problems with drugs and alcohol, problems with the law, being a troubled teen, running away from home or foster home, being kicked out of their home or school, or merely having no interest in school.

Military Service

A common path for those that did not finish high school, and a number of others in the sample, included military service. A 1993 county health department study estimated that approximately 25 percent of the Plainview's homeless were military veterans (Urban Development Department 1996). In a study of twenty-four major cities, veteran status among the homeless was estimated at 11 percent (U.S. Conference of Mayors 2006). Fifteen of the forty-five informants (33.3 percent) mentioned military service. In comparison, approximately 19 percent of males eighteen to sixty-four years of age and older had military experience (U.S. Bureau of the Census 2000). One informant reached the rank of captain but the rest of the informants served in the enlisted ranks and were only in the service for a few years. Three of the men did not serve their original commitment to the military because they were discharged for disciplinary problems.

When discussing military service, a number of men expressed regret for not having turned the military into a career. Many of these men would now be eligible for retirement had they stayed in the military. Besides the three men who were dishonorably discharged, the main reason offered for not continuing with their military career was because that was never the men's intent. The majority of men explained their military service as a way to get out of their family situation, to escape trouble with the local law, or because they had quit school and did not have anything else they wanted to do. Don's explanation represents all three of these reasons:

> I got in some trouble with the law and they jerked me out of school and threw me in jail for about four months. They put me in like in October and I got out in February. That blew two fucking semesters (at a community college). It totally wrecked the whole fucking year. And I was pissed off. I fucked around for about six months. Then me and my mom got into it. She said you either go back to school, get a job, or join the Army. So I said, "Fuck it." I was half looped so I went down and enlisted. I signed up for two years and I would have been there longer but I guess it was April of 1975 when Saigon fell. So then the Army really started pulling out. So the Army came in and told us that they have half a million men that we don't know what to do with. The Army has layoffs too.

Paul was an Air Force air traffic controller before volunteering for two tours in Vietnam as a rescue helicopter pilot. He was promoted to the rank of captain before returning to civilian life as an air traffic controller. He explained that his military service had nothing to do with his current bout of homelessness, but the link between homelessness and veterans is a common theme in the research (i.e., Tessler et al. 2003; Gamache, Rosenheck, and Tessler 2003). According to Paul, military experience during Vietnam had influenced many of his friends on the street: "There are a lot of vets out here. There are a lot of vets that just can't handle staying in one place and big crowds. A lot of them I know are tired of society. What has society done for them? Ha! Stepped on them."

Troubles with the Law

The common thread of trouble with the law has already surfaced in previous discussions. More specifically, almost all informants discussed at least limited trouble with the law and thirteen had spent time in jail. The reasons for jail sentences ranged from the accumulation of multiple misdemeanor tickets to murder. The main theme to surface for jail time, and general trouble with the law, dealt with drugs and alcohol. These experiences ranged from Don who estimated that he had received fifty tickets in Plainview, most for open container or public intoxication, to serious time spent in jail for drug possession and violent crimes. When someone had amassed as many tickets as Don, the police often picked them up for failure to appear in court or failure to pay their fines. At this point the offender had two options, either to pay all their tickets or sit in jail earning credit towards their fine. Jail time was the option most homeless were forced to take.

Don's frequent contact with the law was not unusual. Homeless individuals are most often charged with violations such as loitering, public intoxication, and disorderly conduct that reflect their marginal status in society (Lee and Schreck 2005). Attempting behaviors that are routine, but are typically conducted in private spaces, such as sleeping, resolving disputes, attending to bodily functions, etc. expose the homeless to greater attention and scrutiny from public officials (Snow and Mulcahy 2001; Snow et al. 1989). This greater attention, typically manifesting itself in the form of city policies designed to criminalize and ultimate drive away street living, led Knowles (2000) to refer to the homeless as "walking exiles."

On a level of hardship, jail time like that described by Don was relatively easy to overcome. Hard time, however, left a scar on many of these men. When asked what types of people they refuse to partner up with or hang around, a number of men stated that they avoided people with no respect for the law. Tommy, now forty-two years old and homeless, spent thirteen years in prison for murder. He refused to associate with anyone without respect for the law because he "will never do another day in jail."

Craig, a thirty-eight year-old drug addict and alcoholic, has already had five heart attacks. After three DUIs he was caught driving on a suspended license. This offense resulted in a lifelong suspension and two and a half years in the state penitentiary. He used to view getting from point A to point B while screwed up as a game. After his prison time he no longer has that attitude.

> It's not a game. I ain't doing no more time. Two and a half years is a long time. I pretty much lost everything when I went to prison. My second wife, two kids, an old pickup truck, a couple cars, a house, garage, and dogs. I got out of prison with two boxes of clothes and a Mr. Coffee. And the coffeepot broke when it got delivered to me. I lost it all. That is another reason why I am kind of the way I am now.

Craig is a prime example of the impact incarceration could have on an ex-con. When discussing the broken Mr. Coffee, tears filled his eyes. At the time of the interview he carried everything he owned in a backpack which never left his sight. Given his fear of losing everything again and the potential impact of such a traumatic event, as well as the higher rates of crime within the homeless community (Lee and Schreck 2005), Craig's actions seemed to be warranted.

Health Concerns

Homelessness is bad for a person's health. Tuberculosis, generally thought to be an illness of developing countries, and AIDS run can be found among the homeless (Wright 1990). In addition to such feared illnesses, the homeless face higher levels of infectious disease, mental illness, injury, substance abuse, nutritional deficiencies, and a host of other ailments (Burt et al. 2001). There are also conditions clearly associated with the homeless lifestyle. For instance, the accumulation of fluid in legs and feet, leading to edema, cellulites, and in extreme cases, gangrene, are often a result of being forced to stand in lines for every meal and to sleep sitting up (Wright 1990).

Interviews did not include discussions of tuberculosis or AIDS but general issues of health, both physical and mental, were most certainly mentioned as sources of concern among the informants. Physically, these men have led a hard life. It not only showed in their faces but also in the comments regarding their ability to work. Many of the men cited numerous physical ailments that kept them from working full-time jobs. From Craig's five heart attacks to chronic back problems resulting from years of hard labor, the ailments ran the gamut.

Mental health problems also kept many of the men from working or maintaining jobs. The most commonly cited problems stemmed from depression. All of the informants that discussed their problems with depression talked about not having the strength to get out of bed on some mornings. Trevor, like so many homeless, suffers from both physical and mental health problems. Trevor spoke of why he could not get a job:

I have a lung problem. It is called Chronic Obstructive Pulmonary Disease. I also suffer from depression. I take medication for both of them. I can't pass a physical. The minute I get a job they take me out and send me to a physical and they do a drug test. Then I have to tell them what I am on and why. Then I am either over qualified or under qualified. I worked ten years in the defense industry and six years for the railroad. I've got a wealth of experience but I can't get a job. I've got a bag over on the other side (The Living Room). I'll show you. I've got my social security printouts and everything. I made $35,000 a year when that was big money. I ran a farm for twenty years. I had my own farm. My kids have it now. I applied for SSI and they turned me down. They said right in it (the application) that I have emphysema. They admit I suffer from depression, a chemical lack in my brain. Like I said, I can sit here for two weeks and just stare at the walls. Not eat. I have the blackest thoughts you could imagine. I would work if they would give me a job. But nobody is going to give me a job.

Patterns of Work

Despite the inability of many informants to work regularly, the majority of the sample, including those with physical and mental restrictions, did work. Their work patterns may have been sporadic, and there were a few who simply refused to work, but the common stereotype of lazy bums was not at all fitting. Issue could be taken with that stereotype for two reasons. First, as Don explained, being homeless is a full time job:

Let me tell you, living on the streets is a job. It is a full-time job. Sometimes I have had choices of whether I could go to work or find something to eat. I had no money so I could go to work all day and go hungry or hang out where I can get something to eat. What are you going to do? People think it is easy to skip meals. You don't see a lot of fat people on the street. They are usually very lean. You are constantly on the go.

Sumerlin (1996) explained that the homeless need to adapt to life on the street much the same way people prepare for a career. The daily survival skills needed by homeless to secure the basic necessities of life must be developed and adapted for the situation. Snow and Anderson (1993) explain that over time, the homeless develop daily routines that aid them in securing food, clothing, shelter and other basic needs. These routines tend to take a significant amount of individual's time and energy.

Not only does keeping warm and fed take an extraordinary amount of energy, living on the street makes it incredibly difficult to get and maintain a job. Parker, a forty-four year-old loner, was kicked out of his house, and the lives of his ex-wife and kids, on Christmas day 1987. He has been homeless since. He identified how getting and maintaining a job is difficult without a home.

I'm trying to straighten my life but it is not easy. Once you dig yourself that hole, it is pretty hard to get out of. It is the little things. Say you are trying to get a job and you are camped out by the mission (where he camps). If you don't stay there, they are not going to let you take a shower. Ok, now say that you get a job even washing dishes during the daytime. This place (The Living Room) only has showers during the daytime. So if you're working daytimes and you're not staying at the mission, there is no place to clean up. And if you don't clean yourself up, you're not going to have a job.

The second reason the lazy bum stereotype was not warranted was because the work histories of many of these men, before their bouts of homelessness, were quite extensive. Pre-homeless incomes ranged from Paul's $85,000 to Don who had always gone to day labor when he "wasn't too messed up." Work experiences were also quite varied. From Chris's twenty years spent working on offshore oil rigs to Craig's claim that he had fifty jobs on file at the Social Security office, informants have not spent their entire lives unemployed.

Even during episodes, or literally decades of homelessness, these men survived by working. Informants typically brought in money by working for day labor pools, waiting by the mission for construction supervisors to recruit them each morning, selling plasma, flying a sign, recycling discarded items, or engaging in illegal activities. Illegal activities generally included the selling of drugs and petty larceny. Snow and Anderson (1993) thoroughly examined ways in which the homeless participate in the work force. They concluded that homeless engage in what can be referred to as shadow work. Four categories of shadow work were identified by Snow and Anderson (1993), including selling and trading, soliciting donations in public places, scavenging, and theft. The work may not be consistent and what is traditionally thought of as a job, but this population did work. As Don pointed out to one of his brothers who called him a bum, "The only way I know how to drink is to work for it. I just don't work the way you work."

Conclusion

The descriptive nature of this study leads to two stories, one of commonality and one of distinction. In terms of commonality, it was clear that road dogs and loners did not exist in two separate worlds. During the interviews informants discussed traits, characteristics, and experiences that were common among both road dogs and loners. They are obviously homeless and poor but also faced similar problems of dependency, involvement in the legal system, military backgrounds, educational deficits, health related concerns, few people they can turn to for support, and sporadic patterns of work. These are the experiences that characterized life on the street. These findings were supported by a number of previous studies on the general homeless population (i.e., Canton et al. 2005;

Tessler et al. 2003, Jackson-Wilson and Borgers 1993; Reiley 1993; Snow and Anderson 1993; Sterk-Elifson and Elifson 1992).

While all informants experienced the bone-chilling cold of the Plainview winters, how they dealt with such hardships was determined in part by the decision to brave it alone or with a partner. These differences were the crux of this examination, and the story of distinction. Loners and road dogs may live on the same streets, frequent the same shelters, and brave the same winters, but having someone to turn to provided for very different adaptations to life on the street.

One of the main differences between road dogs and loners was indicated through an examination of their level of affiliation (La Gory et al. 1991). Not surprisingly, loners had lower levels of affiliation than road dogs. This major distinction between the two groups was also apparent throughout the interviews. Road dogs, unlike loners, spent much of their time running with another homeless man. These partnerships were formed because they sought companionship, common goals, and the desire to make life on the streets more bearable. Partnering up based on common goals included travel destinations, seeking work, or the acquisition of drugs or alcohol. Overall, road dogs typically cited that partnering up made survival on the streets easier.

While road dogs typically cited partnerships as necessary for survival, loners demonstrated that such partnerships were not essential for everyone. Ultimately, road dogs and loners demonstrated different strategies for survival on the street. Instead of taking a running mate, loners preferred a strategy of only relying on themselves. Some informants simply said they did not partner up or have many friends because they "were simply a loner," but the majority of informants cited issues of trust, nuisance, and mental health. Most loners cited that they did not feel they could trust other homeless men, they did not want to be bothered, or in the case of Don, mental illness created problems with forming interpersonal relationships.

Chapter Four

Brother, Can You Spare a Dime?

From Whence They Came

Tragic events such as unemployment, divorce, death of a spouse or parent, substance abuse, and imprisonment happen to millions of men and women in the United States each year. The vast majority of these events, however, do not lead to homelessness. When people do find themselves to be homeless it is typically after a series of tough breaks and because they have exhausted or never had sufficient resources to keep them housed. The most important and effective social institution at keeping its members from living on the street is the family. Family safety nets of financial and emotional support are what keep the ranks of the homeless from exploding on a daily basis.

In the case of most informants, the safety nets provided by members of the men's families of origin were weak or nonexistent. Listening to informants describe their childhood was one of the most difficult tasks of the research. The interview transcripts read like a series of case studies detailing family separation, abandonment, death, alcoholism, and abuse. For example, Eric, a thirty-year-old tramp from Philadelphia identified why he was not able to remain in his hometown and what role his family plays in his current situation:

> My dad left when I was five years old. He left my mom for a sixteen-year-old kid. I grew up in an alcoholic environment. All my family including my uncles and aunts, everybody, are alcoholics. I turned out to be an alcoholic myself. And of course it has an effect on me and the position I am in because I would probably still be in Philadelphia if I had a place to go.

In examining these situations, this chapter will address the roles that families of origin played in the lives of the homeless informants. Road dogs and loners will be compared in relation to family backgrounds and contact with families of origin. In addition, exchanges of both tangible and intangible support between informants and their families of origin will be assessed. Doing so will set the stage for a theoretical discussion of exchanges between informants and both families of creation and origin in Chapter Six.

For the majority of the informants, like Eric, from whence they came was not ideal. Of the forty-five informants, twenty-eight experienced the death of at least one parent or stepparent, nine spent a considerable amount of time in foster homes, orphanages, group homes, or with relatives other than their parents, and five had parents who had been sent to prison or mental institutions. Most of the informants also witnessed the divorce or separation of their parents, abandonment by their biological fathers, or multiple stepparents. Because of the complexity and pain associated with disrupted family ties, a few found these issues difficult to talk about. When Ben, a thirty-eight-year-old road dog, was asked about his family he simply stated, "I haven't seen them in twenty years and I cannot take you back that far." He refused to elaborate any further. The vast majority of the informants, however, offered detailed information about their families of origin and their current relationships.

Shared Experiences

Analysis of the data revealed several themes regarding experiences that were common among informants. Almost all of the respondents discussed families of origin that had serious disruptions and problems and only a few claimed to have good relationships with at least one parent at the time of the interview. While the data do not allow for a causal link between the informants' current states of homelessness and their families of origin, the family histories of these men cannot be ignored. What was particularly interesting was that even among the few respondents who described their relationships as good or close, they too typically had very limited contact with family members.

The following section identifies the themes of shared experiences of the homeless men in the study. These shared experiences include physical abuse, alcoholic parents, poverty, and family separation. These results are consistent with other studies that find high levels of family instability and conflict (i.e., Canton et al. 2005; Reilly 1993). Dealing with troubling family issues repeatedly meant that as youth, informants had to deal with multiple stepparents, institutionalized care, or an absence of care.

Alcoholism and Abuse. The role alcohol played in the lives of these men has already been visited a number of times. Problems with drugs and alcohol affected many men in the sample and these problems often began before they even took their first hit or drink. Trevor, described by a Living Room employee as a raging alcoholic, had been on and off the street since the late 1980s. When asked to describe the family he grew up with, he recounted:

I had two brothers and two sisters. One brother is already dead. Both of my parents are dead. My father was an alcoholic, my mother was an alcoholic, and I am an alcoholic. My brother is an alcoholic. I have one sister who is normal. The other sister is a pill junkie. There was physical abuse and emotional abuse, but there is always that kind of environment. Very seldom do you find families that are not dysfunctional when they have alcoholic parents.

As evident from Trevor's observations, in most of the cases parental alcoholism and physical abuse went hand in hand. Ed, a fifty-three-year-old loner, spent most of his time isolating himself from other people and has lived in his van for years. He also experienced a childhood with these two obstacles:

My dad was an alcoholic. He used to beat my mom. For some reason I was his favorite. My older brother was my half brother. My dad couldn't stand him. He used to make us fight. He used to make me beat him up. He used to say if I didn't beat him up, he was going to beat him up. He (half brother) had a baby duck. I remember this very well. My dad cut off his head and threw it in the garbage. I had a pet parakeet. My dad let him out of the cage. I don't know how he knew this, but we had an old-fashioned stove where you put wood in the bottom. He (dad) lifted the burner plate up and the bird flew right in. I don't know how he knew the bird would do that, but he did. He was a very cruel man. When I was sixteen I broke my father's jaw. That probably ain't nice, but I hate him. I despise him. I hate my dad. I haven't seen him since I was sixteen. He came to where we lived and knocked on the door (after Ed's mom kicked him out). I looked at him and hit him with everything I had. He got up and walked out. That was the last time I ever seen him.

Similarly, when studying homeless youth, Tyler et al. (2000), Solarz (1988), and others found that in addition to physical and sexual abuse, the homes they ran from, or were thrown out of, were characterized by high levels of conflict, discipline problems, and lack of affection. With this study, not only did alcoholism and abuse seem to exist as a pair, alcoholism and poverty also tended to operate hand-in-hand for many informants.

Poverty. A few of the informants came from financially stable, even wealthy families, but the majority of the respondents described the financial situations while growing up as quite tenuous. For example, Eric grew up in a Philadelphia neighborhood famous for its poverty. "I come from a poor, alcoholic, drug addict family. I grew up at Third and Jackson in Philadelphia. It is considered the Kensington section where they filmed the *Rocky* movies. That's my neighborhood where I grew up."

Despite the high level of poverty among informants' families of origin, no respondent had parents who were or had been homeless. Most men simply described their situations as living with hand-me downs and doing without expensive toys. There are plenty of tales of economic hardship, but the real issue is not that most of these men had humble beginnings, but the complex situations that surrounded their financial backgrounds. As previously stated, the majority of informants experienced incidents of parental death, divorce, or institutionalization.

Family Separation: Death, Divorce, Abandonment, Institutionalization, and Single Parenting. The most pervasive theme when analyzing the shared family experiences of the informants was the exposure to family disruption. Over half of the respondents were raised for a considerable amount of time by only one parent because of parental death, divorce, abandonment, or institutionalization. Twenty-eight (62 percent) of the respondents mentioned the death of at least one parent. Of the twenty-eight, sixteen had parents die when they were young. This is in addition to the numerous men who felt abandoned after a losing contact with a parent after a divorce or who never had contact with parents. Seventeen (38 percent) respondents experienced at least one parental divorce during their childhood. An additional sixteen never knew, or lost contact with one or both of their biological parents following the parental separation. As described by the men, the consequences of such family disruption were often quite tragic.

Family ties were also weakened because of parental institutionalization. Four informants had fathers who spent time in prison and one of the respondents had a mother who was placed in a mental hospital. After John's parents were divorced and his dad left, his mother was sent to the "nuthouse." As a result, John, now in his fifties, not only found himself in foster care, but also separated from his siblings. John has been homeless and living on the streets of the same city since 1970. When I asked him to describe his family, John elaborated:

> It is like a dysfunctional family. Broken home thing. My parents got divorced (when he was five years old) and me, Tim, and Tonya went to one foster home. My two other brothers went to a foster farm. Boy did they hate it down there. All I had to do was go to school. (After the divorce) my mom went to Green Hill Hospital, which is a nuthouse. And the old man, he went somewhere. I don't know.

According to informants, parental death, divorce, abandonment and institutionalization have created major rifts in their families of origin. In each of these situations major obstacles have been erected that diminish the possibility of maintaining contact with families of origin. The fallout of such family experiences, as assessed by contact between the men and their families of origin, will be examined shortly. Before contact can be discussed, how these issues were dealt with must be examined. In response to family disruption, many informants were exposed to multiple stepparents, foster homes, and having to grow up alone.

The Complexities of Family Life

Stepparents. Of the twelve informants who lived with a stepparent, eleven were stepfathers. It was not unusual for informants to live with more than one stepfather while growing up. Living with more than one stepparent was a result of multiple remarriages or being shuffled between biological parents. Kent, a nineteen-year-old drug addict, lived with both his father and mother after his parents divorced when he was six. He described his family in the following way:

> I got one half-sister because before my mom married my dad, my mom got pregnant by this one guy and he took off. My sister never met him. That guy was kind of a dick. So after my mom married my dad I came along. My parents divorced and now since I have a stepdad I have two stepsisters and one step-brother. And my real dad got remarried when I was ten years old so I have two half-brothers.

On the surface, Kent's family seems typical of many post-modern families. He did, however, go on to describe in greater detail the internal dynamics of his family of origin. According to Kent, his mother divorced his father because he had molested Kent's older half-sister. Despite this offense, Kent was sent to live with his father after the divorce. During this time Kent was also molested. After molesting a non-related child, Kent's father was eventually charged and sent to prison.

Among the experiences of the informants with stepparents, there appeared to be two general types of stepparents. There were stepparents who did not get along with their stepchildren, which included abusing them, and there were stepparents who simply did not have much to do with their stepchildren. In the case of Barry, who is fifty-four and became homeless after his wife divorced him in 1984, he had a stepfather who was abusive and eventually caused him to leave his mother.

> The whole thing started when my dad got killed in a farming accident and then my mom remarried. The guy she remarried was a construction worker. They left my hometown and moved to another small town. So I just kind of tagged along. He was the type that if he wasn't drinking he was ok. It was one of those deals where the kids was the problem of all this and of all that. He couldn't face up to his own reality. He always had to push it off on the kids or something else. He could never admit to his own problems. So I went out on my own at 17.

While many of the informants reported abusive stepfathers, many simply did not find any reason to develop a relationship. For instance, Craig plainly did not have anything in common with his stepfather.

> He (father) was a bartender and my mom was a cocktail waitress. I grew up in bars here in town. From 1962 to 1969 it was a pretty stormy marriage. There

was a lot of abuse. My father was an alcoholic. In 1969 they separated. Then in 1970 she remarried. I had a couple of brothers join the family through him. That marriage lasted until 1974. I was moved up to the middle class without an alcoholic father. I was not real comfortable with him (stepfather) because my father went hunting and fishing and my stepfather went to sports games. I was not the sports type. I wasn't a jock. I was a dope addict and a drunk in high school. That is what I learned from my father.

Having a stepparent was not the only possibility for the informants following a family breakup. After experiencing a death, divorce, or abandonment of their patents, nine of the informants were raised for a period of time by people other than biological parents.

Foster Homes, Group Homes, Orphanages, and Other Relatives. Nine (20 percent) of the respondents spent a considerable amount of their youth in foster homes, group homes, orphanages, or with relatives other than their biological parents. These results were similar to those reported by Courtney et al. (2001), Roman and Wolf (1995), Canton, Shrout, Eagle, Opter, Felix, and Dominguez (1994), and Susser et al. (1987).

At the time of the interview, Philip was forty years old and had recently became homeless after a divorce. He was living in Sweden with his wife and two children when his wife divorced him and kicked him out of the house. He returned to the United States but was broke and did not have family to turn to. Philip described a very tragic event that changed his entire life: "I lived with my parents in Indiana. My father was an alcoholic. They both got killed in a car crash. Beyond my two children (in Sweden), all my relatives are dead. He (dad) was a veteran so I was placed in a soldiers and sailors home. There was like five hundred kids there. Way out in the middle of nowhere."

Carter, fifty years old, was conceived during the rape of his then eleven-year-old mother. Carter's mother was living with her parents at the time of the rape. Carter's grandparents took full responsibility for him after his mother moved to Chicago with a man at the age of fifteen. After living a few years in Chicago and having two daughters with her boyfriend, Carter's mother brought him to Chicago to live. Carter explained why this situation did not work:

He (boyfriend) was a very dark-skinned man. In black families there is just a thing where the darker-skinned blacks have an aversion against lighter-skinned blacks. When I was younger, I was light. And my mother is light-skinned. My two sisters were dark-skinned like him so he was ill tempered against me and he would voice his opinion. He would say, "What are you doing with that half-white kid around here." And he was a bit cruel to me and she didn't like it so she sent me back to live with my grandparents.

Jacob, a road dog who had a girlfriend at the time of the interview also had trouble with a stepparent. As a result of the conflict, Jacob was sent to a group home when he was fifteen. According to Jacob, who was being beaten by his stepdad, he was placed in a group home because he was a "stress problem" for his stepdad.

No matter how each of the nine ended up in the care of others the men described the outcomes in similar terms. Contact with any family members was sporadic at best and frequently non-existent. As a result, informants described how these experiences forced them to grow up very quickly.

Growing Up Alone. A common theme found among in the experiences of the informants was that they typically had to fend for themselves. When DJ, a twenty-six-year-old loner, was asked about the family he grew up with he responded, "I haven't grown up that much with them. I have been in and out of foster home deals. I don't know them that well." Growing up alone was also possible while living with parents. Jason, a thirty-nine-year-old loner, described his life with his dad after his parents divorced when he was six:

> My dad was kind of on the mental side. He went to see a psychiatrist because of the marriage breakup and everything. It kind of messed with his head I guess. And he wasn't very emotional. When they split up that is when I had to grow up because I was pretty much on my own. There were no regulations. Sometimes there wasn't even any food. Even though he did make good money because he was retired Air Force. It was almost as if he wasn't there. So basically we had a house but I was on my own. There was no breakfast or lunch. Dinner usually existed, but sometimes it didn't. If there was no dinner you ate whatever was in the refrigerator which was usually empty. I guess he just sort of neglected me. I guess I am sort of like that now because I don't call. I don't have any relationship with my family at all.

On an even more extreme level, Eric, who would still be in Philadelphia if he had a place to go, has been on his own since he was fourteen years old. According to Eric:

> My mom threw me out the door. I've relied on myself ever since. Since I was 12 or 13 she never had to buy clothes for me. She never had to buy sneakers for me. So when she kicked me out the door at fourteen years old, I never went back to live with her. I supported myself. I lived with girlfriends and shit like that. I would say that my family has definitely had an impact, you know, on my situation. My mom never took me to the dentist when I was a kid. That is why my teeth are all fucked up. She was just too busy partying and shit with her friends.

While these themes are disturbing to hear, the experiences among study informants were not unique. Complexities of family life, including out of home placement during childhood, parental instability, and other life-altering events are themes supported by a number of previous studies of homeless adults and youth (i.e., Canton et al. 2005; Herman, Susser, Link, and Struening 1997; Yoder et al. 2001).

Links to the Past

The scope of the data does not allow for a causal link between past family experiences and homelessness, which is fitting given the perspectives of most of the informants. Despite experiencing extensive family turmoil while growing up, past experiences and current situations were rarely linked by the informants. In fact, the comment offered by Eric that his family had an impact on his homelessness was the most direct and yet certainly unrepresentative of the sample. More consistent with the findings of the thematic analysis were conclusions by the men that what they had experienced as youth was relatively typical. According to Parker, a forty-four year-old loner, his childhood was "normal":

> I guess I would have no reason to be where I'm at, the way I am. According to the papers and all the experts, I had a normal childhood I guess. I wasn't abused as a kid, my dad didn't beat me, and he wasn't a drunk. I was born in 1954. I've got a stepsister or a half-sister like seven years older than me. So by the time I was like ten, she was pregnant and gone. So I more or less grew up alone. Didn't have a whole lot of friends. When I was little we moved from town to the country. I never did have a real good relationship with my mother. She slept around a lot. My dad died like a week after I turned 18. I got out of high school, started college and I went to the service. I guess what really ticks me off is my mom and my half-sister are both bitches. I mean, I quit college, went in the service, got out and had nowhere to go. I had worked on the farm. Half the machinery I bought. When I graduated from high school I had $5,000 in the bank. We raised Siberian Husky show dogs. Half of them were registered in my name. Half of the livestock was mine and half of the machinery was mine. While I was in boot camp, mom got married. It hadn't been six months after my dad died. She sold everything and gave the money to him (new husband). She forged my name on all the stuff that was registered and licensed in my name. I have made several attempts since then to get along with her. You know it is great for the first hour or two and then all of the old troubles come up. So that is why I just stay away now.

It has been over ten years since Parker talked to his mother or half-sister and despite his family history he refused to give his kin any credit for his homelessness. This was not uncommon. Despite being kicked out of their homes and other tragic experiences, many informants shared Parker's inability, or refusal, to connect past experiences with current situations. During the interview Ed, whose father was extremely abusive and made a habit of killing family pets, was asked if he saw his family background as a contributing factor as to why he lived in his van. He explained that he did not see a connection. He simply did not see the point in paying someone else to live a house or apartment when he can live in his van and put money in his pocket. He further stressed, "I enjoy my life. I don't have any obligations but to myself and my dog."

Hidden Patterns?

The interview data did not produce any themes that suggested conclusive differences between the structures and experiences of the families of origin of loners and road dogs. Both groups experienced high levels of family separation, issues of substance abuse among kin, poverty, and even abuse, revealing no measurable differences between road dogs and loners. Despite these similarities, it is possible that a larger sample might be able to weed out such differences. An interview with Jason indicated that this might be the case. When asked what made him different from road dogs that seek out partners, Jason responded:

> Possibly the ones that are loners had families who rejected them. The ones that partner up and buddy up maybe the majority of their parents either didn't split up or their parents did take care of them (after the split up). I would say the majority probably, if there was a divorce involved, would have the mother taking care of them (his father took care of him after parent's divorce) and the brothers and sisters all stuck together. They still know each other. Those are the types that can actually buddy together because they have trust. I guess they know what it takes to trust somebody. Me, I don't know how. My parents literally abandoned me. And that is inside of me. I can't trust anyone. I actually search for people, but I can't. I never met anybody that I can trust or be close with. I think that makes the difference. The loners are the ones who literally met rejection from their families, but the buddy types, their mothers or parents showed them some kind of affection or some kind of love. Love can be just feeding you or buying you some clothes, that kind of love. There might not be the kind of love where you're always hugging. But if you've had a lot of hugs you probably tend to hang out in a group and socialize much better.

Jason's comments were not only painful to hear, but also very insightful. While his conclusions were not directly replicated by the data, the survey and demographic results do, at the very least, suggest his observations should receive greater attention. Among the informants' experiences, the percentage of parental divorce and death were similar for road dogs and loners. But when rates of foster care, stepparents, and abandoned were examined, loners registered slightly higher levels. The sample is too small to reach a conclusion in this area. However, Jason's perspective, teamed with the survey data, suggest that this might be fertile area for further research. In addition to Jason's insight, recent studies on homeless and runaway youth could lead to a better understanding of homeless adults who identify as loners. For example, Tyler et al. (2004) argue that dissociative behaviors, which may ultimately have an impact on mental health, may be connected to the neglect, physical abuse, and sexual abuse that many homeless and runaway youth have been exposed to.

Exchanges Between Homeless Men and Their Families of Origin

Family safety nets of financial and emotional support are what keep the ranks of the homeless from exploding on a daily basis. In the case of most study informants, the safety nets provided by families of origin were weak or nonexistent. Data from both interviews ($N = 45$) and surveys ($n = 35$) were used to document the level of exchange between homeless men and their families of origin. Exchanges were separated into two separate categories, intangible and tangible exchanges. Within intangible exchanges, evidence of low levels of information sharing and emotional support were found. Tangible exchanges, recorded at extremely low levels, included housing, financial assistance, food, and clothing.

Intangible Exchanges

Intangible items, by their very definition, are hard to identify. This challenge to the research design led to the examination of contact between the homeless men and their families of origin. Level of contact is important because it can be measured and the emotional connections and exchanges of information identified by informants were described as the main reason for contacting their relatives.

Contact with members of the men's family of origin was measured in two ways. First, it was assessed with direct questions in the interviews. Secondly, contact was measured through three questions on the affiliation survey. The three questions asked, "Do you visit, talk to, or write your parents/brothers or sisters/other relatives at least once every two or three months." As reported in Chapter Three, the survey data indicated higher level of overall affiliation for road dogs, but did not reveal any major differences between road dogs and loners in terms of contact with relatives. Of those that had living parents, about half the loners and road dogs talked to, wrote, or visited with their parents at least once every two to three months. When the same question was asked of siblings and other relatives, only about one-third of both road dogs and loners had contact with relatives other than their parents. The interview data, however, did reveal differences between the level and type of contact with families of origin. On the whole, road dogs were, according to interview data, more likely to have contact with their families of origin than were loners.

Overall Frequency of Informational and Emotional Exchanges. The sample was not totally isolated from their families of origin, but the majority of respondents had very little or no contact with their families of origin. This finding is consistent with other research on affiliation between homeless adults and family members. For example, Rossi (1990) reported that less than half of the homeless individuals in the study maintained contact with their families. During interviews for this study, informants frequently responded, "It is ok" or "Pretty good" when asked, "What kind of relationship do you have with your parents/siblings right now?" After probing to find out the last time they talked with any members of their families, it was not unusual to have them respond that it had been several years since they had any contact.

Based on interview data, twenty-one informants (47 percent) had no contact with anyone from their families of origin in over a year. Of the twenty-four informants (53 percent) that reported some level of contact, sixteen had sporadic contact ranging from a call or visit at Christmas to checking in every few months. The modal level of contact for this group was approximately once every six months. The remaining eight (18 percent) were rated as having a consistent level of contact. The contact may have only been once a month, which was the modal level for the group rated as having consistent contact, but it was on a relatively regular basis throughout the year. According to informants, contact with families of origin did create the possibility for the exchange of tangible resources, but most contact was for the purpose of maintaining emotional connections and exchanges of information.

Contact was also assessed through survey data ($n = 35$) by asking respondents if they visit with, talk to, or write their parents at least every two or three months (La Gory et al. 1991). A second question asked about contact with siblings. In terms of contact with members of their families of origin, only twelve (34 percent) expressed that they typically had contact with their parents at least every two or three months. Ten respondents (29 percent) reported sibling contact at least every two or three months.

The survey also asked if a relative had given the respondent money, food, clothing, housing, a ride, advice, or listened to their troubles in the year prior to the interview. It should be noted that this question asked about all relatives, so distinctions cannot be made between the two family types being compared. The most common type of support offered by family of origin members, as indicated through interview data, was advice or listening to the troubles of the informants, representing likely examples of emotional exchanges taking place. Survey data indicated that seventeen of the thirty-five informants (49 percent) were beneficiaries of such support. In comparison, ten informants (29 percent) had received food and clothing, and fourteen (40 percent), mostly the same informants, had received a ride in the past year. These results reflect a recurring theme throughout the research, with informants more likely to occasionally check in with relatives and share information than ask for a substantial level of tangible support.

Beyond the general theme expressed by informants that there simply should be contact between relatives, additional explanations for contact between homeless men and their families of origin were offered. The first reason was to exchange information or seek emotional connections. One of the primary outcomes of this exchange was to let family members know that they were alive and doing okay. For example, Coulter's mom passed away when he was sixteen years old, he never knew his biological father, and he did not get along with his stepfather so there were few kin that Coulter could contact. He did have two brothers and a sister that he called a couple of times a year to "Let them know I am alive and see what they are doing."

It was also somewhat common for tramps to stop by a relative's home when they were traveling. While he did not want to see his mother, Craig felt the need to keep his mother informed of his whereabouts. Ultimately, Craig ended up telling his mother more than he planned and believed he should:

> She would rather not see my lifestyle. Out of sight, out of mind. That is kind of the reason why I am up here in the city doing what I want to. I call her and I swear I am not going to tell her but I have to. I have to be truthful with her. I end up telling her that I got booted out of a place and I am living on the street, but I am ok. I am surviving. I call her up at least once a month and sometimes every two weeks. I have always been honest with my mom.

Craig's calls to his mother represent one of the most consistent themes found when assessing levels of contact between informants and their relatives. Contact with mothers was much more likely than with any family or origin or creation. This finding will be addressed more completely in Chapter Six.

Loners. When asked about specific contact during the interviews, loners were less likely to have consistent contact with members of their families of origin than were road dogs. Only five loners reported any contact with parents or siblings within the past few years. Of the five, only two had what could be considered close contact. Sandy, now thirty-one years old, stopped going to school in the eighth grade. He considered his parents the most important people in his life and tried to keep contact with them. The contact that he described took place about once a month and was over the phone. Just prior to the interview, his mom tried to get Sandy to return for his cousin's wedding but he told her that he could not make it. While keeping in contact with his parents was important, he, like many informants, preferred talking by phone rather than visiting in person.

James, a fifty-four-year-old pool shark, was the only other loner who claimed consistent and close contact with members of his family of origin. James called his mother, who also lived in the same city, once a week but he was not, as he described, close with her or any other family member. James described his family as not very helpful:

> I come from a rich family but it doesn't matter. Even if you are out on the streets starving and everything, they will not give you a five-dollar bill. They are real uppity-up. They could have one thousand dollars in their pocket and you couldn't get a meal out of them. I see them (mom and siblings) just once every Christmas. Mom begs me to come, so I come. That is the only time I see any of them.

It was evident from talking to the self-described loners that they were not selective loners. That is, they were typically distant not only from other homeless, but even from their families of origin. Although many road dogs were also found to be quite distant from their families of origin, interview data indicated that there was a higher proportion found among the loners.

Road Dogs. Based on interview data, nineteen of the thirty-three road dogs had some level of contact with members of their family of origin in the year prior to the interview. Fourteen road dogs reported that they had no contact with any such relative. Of the nineteen road dogs that were in contact with members of their families of origin, twelve had sporadic contact ranging from a call or visit on holidays to checking in every few months. The remaining seven were rated as having a consistent level of contact.

Although there were exceptions like Jerry, a thirty-eight-year-old tramp who frequently went back home to care for his aging parents, most of the seven road dogs with regular contact kept in touch by phone. This theme was also apparent among the loners. Paul, fifty-two years old, called his parents and his adult children once or twice a month. Paul owned a construction company until two years prior to his interview. Paul had been an Air Force pilot, an air traffic controller, and most recently a general contractor. His wife's bout with stomach cancer, and eventual death, drained him of his personal and business assets. When interviewed he lived under a bridge with Coulter, a thirty-five-year-old rail tramp. Paul's children were financially stable professionals and his parents are quite wealthy, but he retreated to the streets after tiring of friends and relatives constantly expressing their sympathy to him. According to Paul, he needed his space to work through this loss on his own and until then his contact with his family would be by phone.

According to Paul, his family appreciates his contact and wished they could do more, but that was not the case of all informants. Craig, an alcoholic and drug addict, only called his mother because he would rather she not see his lifestyle. He was less worried about his brother's reaction. A few times a year Craig showed up drunk at his brother's house in the middle of the night just to say, "Hey bro, what's happening?" Needless to say, Craig knew his brother did not appreciate his visits.

Tangible Exchanges

Most people see their family as a place to turn in times of need, but a considerable number of Americans are not able to rely on their families of origin. A small number of informants had very supportive families that would do anything to get them off the street, but most road dogs and loners were frequently unable to rely on their family for support and had little to offer as part of an exchange-based relationship.

Exchanges of tangible support between informants and their families of origin were assessed through both interview and survey data. When taking the affiliation survey, respondents were asked if any relative in the past year had given them food, advice, money, clothes, a place to stay, a ride, or taken care of them while they were sick. This measure did not differentiate between informants staying only one night or receiving only one ride during the past year with a family member from informants who regularly called upon relatives for assistance. Mean levels of support from relatives in general (Cronbach's Alpha = .892) were found to be 1.30 (sd = 2.36) for loners and 2.76 (sd = 2.57) for road dogs.

Informants' perceived level of support was also assessed in the interviews. Respondents were asked if they could count on, or would seek, support from their families of origin if they became injured and were no longer able to survive on the street. Informants were also asked about actual support, however, the main focus was on if these men could turn to a relative if their situation became even more disastrous than it already was. Similar to the survey results, the interview data found higher levels of support and perceived support among road dogs.

Housing. The most common type of tangible support discussed in the interviews was temporary housing. According to Marin and Vacha (1994), the numbers of homeless would swell drastically if relatives and friends were not able to double up. Marin and Vacha (1994) studied two hundred residentially at risk persons receiving energy assistance and found that 82 percent reported doubling up with friends and relatives in the last year. Of those doubling up, around 60 percent were doubling up with relatives. Among the thirty-five informants who completed the survey, thirteen (37 percent) were allowed to stay with relatives at least once during the past year. Even though the survey did not distinguish between families of origin and creation, interview data did not reveal any instances where informants stayed with created family members.

Staying with relatives was typically not a long-term solution but rather an occasional respite from the streets. In most cases, temporary housing was exchanged for household labor or rent assistance, but this was not always the case. For example, DJ occasionally crashed at his sister's house. DJ identified how this support was limited because of his inability to provide anything in return: "I don't like to worry all the time. I like to kick back and relax too. That is why sometimes I go to my sister's house. That is what I usually do there, kick back. But I can't stay long because it isn't my house. I ain't paying no bills. It is just a place I can go get cleaned up and go on my way."

In some cases, informants were able to have a longer respite from the streets, often based on relationships of exchange, but never developing into long-term solutions. Interview data revealed that 18 percent of informants had gone back home to live with their parents for a short time or had been taken in by a sibling or other relative within the past few years. The majority of these arrangements lasted from a few days to a few weeks, never lasting more than three months. Many of these experiences ended in hard feelings. Randy, a forty-seven-year-old tramp, stayed with his cousin when he first became homeless because his sister would not take him in. He explained how the arrangement was terminated when he was no longer able to fulfill his end of the exchange relationship:

> I was homeless but I had never actually had to stay in the mission or on the streets. I was staying with my cousin and working through temp work. The work was steady and I was making good money, paying my cousin rent, and saving money for a place of my own. Then I fell in the bathtub and ruptured a disk in my back. It was pinching up against the main nerve causing extreme pain (he could no longer work). And I guess because my cousin was going through a divorce and she was under extreme stress. The two of us lost our tempers and she kicked me out. I have been homeless and on the streets since then.

In a few cases, there had always been somewhere to go home. Four of the forty-five men (9 percent) contended that their families were always willing to take them in but they choose not to accept the invitation. In the case of Jerry it was his street friends and a call to the road that kept him from staying too long with his parents. Jerry explained that he frequently traveled to his hometown to check on and help his aging parents. He typically spent a week or two making sure they are doing okay and helping them with household chores and maintenance.

> They (family) have done everything they could to get me off the streets. When I leave they ask, "Why are you going back to Plainview?" I tell them that I just want to see my friends, you know. They know good and well that I am going to go back down to the streets and the railroad yards, holding signs and stuff. But they don't say nothing. You can take the tramp off the streets, but you can't take the streets out of the tramp.

Jerry's situation demonstrates not only an exchange of temporary housing for domestic labor, but also a likely example of more intangible exchanges such as emotional support.

Financial Aid. The second form of tangible exchanges included the receipt of financial aid. In the interviews, only a few informants spoke of direct financial aid from their families of origin and only eleven (31 percent) of those completing the survey had received monetary aid in the year prior to the study. Those that did often mentioned, as with Craig, that the aid was something that would no longer be offered because the informants had blown the money on drugs or alcohol. Other times the support was simply a few bills pulled out of a wallet at the end of a visit. Randy mentioned an offering of money from his sister that he found very odd. "On Thanksgiving my sister came down here (Grace Kitchen) and gave me two packs of cigarettes and five dollars. After she handed it to me she said, 'Hopefully that will keep you off the sidewalk.' I can't explain that. I was grateful so I said thank you and just shut up."

Beyond direct financial offerings, family members would occasionally strike an exchange between homeless sons who would perform odd jobs around the home for compensation. This type of exchange was previously demonstrated by Jerry. When housing was not offered, the typical pattern was for a homeless son to be given payment to repair something around the house for his divorced or widowed mother. Troy, a thirty-seven-year-old home guard (homeless individuals who rarely travel and are long-term residents of a community), was using the fact that his mother needed some help around the house as a way to repair the relationship.

> I had such a bad year last year. I was depressed all the time. I didn't see her (his mom) and it turned out she needed a handyman. I am a handyman and she was trying to get in contact with me but I didn't call her. I feel real bad. We got together earlier this year. I met my step dad. It was the first time I saw her in over a year. She was mad. I don't know how long she had been mad but she was mad. She has disowned both of her sons. As far as she was concerned, she had no children (her youngest son had died and Troy and another brother had abandoned her). She didn't want nothing to do with her family, but we are working on it. I am going over there this weekend. I am going to rebuild her bathroom. She had someone do it last summer but they didn't do it right. So it needs to be redone and I am going to go over there this weekend and get it done right. I told her when she said she disowned me that I haven't disowned her. I am doing everything that I can to be a good son. That's what I am in the process of doing now.

Troy's example demonstrates the difficulty of separating tangible and intangible exchanges taking place between family members. Even though Troy was compensated for his labor, his carpentry skills served as a way to connect more with his mother.

Conclusion

Results, especially those derived from survey data, indicate that the majority of the informants lacked family safety nets, at least in part, because of their family histories. It was discovered that the family backgrounds of these men were typically quite troubling. As youth, many informants experienced a childhood in poverty, with alcoholic parents, were subject to violence, and witnessed the disorganization of their family unit for a variety of reasons. Despite these common themes, informants did not openly blame their relationships with their families of origin for their homelessness.

It was also discovered that while not totally isolated, the majority of the adult informants were not able, or refused, to rely on consistent contact and support from their families of origin. Overall, exchange-based relationships were rare, with intangible exchanges such sharing information being the most prevalent. Tangible exchanges, even more rare, typically encompassed financial help and housing assistance. In relation to the types of exchanges that took place, as well as the reasons for entering into such arrangements, road dogs and loners appeared to be more similar than different.

The one difference that presented itself was in relation to the actual levels of contact and exchange. When loners and road dogs were compared, interview data revealed slightly higher rates of contact and exchange among road dogs. Loners, on the other hand, were more likely to express that they did not need help from anyone. The theory put forth by Jason, concerning the possibility that loners suffered higher levels of abandonment, is certainly an area that needs greater examination. A second area that also needs attention will be the focus of Chapter Six. After examining the rates and types of intangible and tangible exchanges that took place between informants and created kin in Chapter Five, explanations for the level and type of exchanges between informants and their families will be sought. Social exchange and gender theories will be utilized as a framework for the discussion.

Chapter Five

Ex-Wife, Can You Spare a Dime?

The Creation and Disruption of Family Relationships

Relationship structure, contact, and exchanges of tangible and intangible support between informants and their created kin were evaluated through interview data. The affiliation survey did not directly address created families. The term created kin is being used to describe the spouses and children of the informants. Girlfriends were also counted as created kin if they had produced a child with the informant. Fictive kin, also arguably "created" relationships, entail different types of relationships and will be discussed in the chapter addressing road dogs.

Like their relationships with biological and adopted families, informants described fragmented and nonexistent ties to their created kin. Informants also offered similar reasons for contact or lack of ties with their created families. In the ensuing sections, the extent of created kin will be described in addition to the nature of both intangible and tangible exchanges. Of the forty-five respondents, twenty-six (58 percent) had never been married and twenty (44 percent) did not have any children. In relation to marital status, three (7 percent) were married at the time of the interview (only one was not separated) and sixteen (36 percent) respondents were divorced or widowers. These men did not spend their time on the streets with their created kin.

Past and Present Marriages

Current Unions. TC, a thirty-five-year-old rail tramp, was the only informant who was married and not separated. TC had been homeless for the majority of the past twelve years, and met his wife, Kathy, about eight years prior to the interview. TC was traveling around the country by freight train when he landed in Topeka, Kansas in 1991. He met Kathy in a mission after she has lost her job selling magazines door to door. Shortly after meeting, they were married, moved back to her home state of Virginia, found an apartment, and had a child who died of Sudden Infant Death Syndrome (SIDS). Kathy and TC eventually had two more children but they live with Kathy's aunt in Virginia. TC revealed their decision:

> We were paying rent (in Virginia) but the cost of living is so high and the pay scale is so low. It brought us back into the same situation we were in when we met. That's why we decided that it is best for our children to be in a more stable environment with Kathy's aunt than out on the streets until we get ourselves more financially stable.

After leaving their children with Kathy's aunt, they began traveling. Six months later they landed in Plainview. Since then they camped out in a tent or under a bridge every night and hoped to reach the top of the HUD housing list. TC did not know when he would be able to see his children again, let alone take custody of them, but he did call them on a weekly basis. Kathy and TC's relationship was not classified as a road dog relationship. Their legal ties, parental status, and sexual nature of the relationship made their situation distinct from street partnerships between two men. More importantly, TC did not consider Kathy his road dog. TC has had many road dogs and maintained a significant relationship with his most recent traveling partner. Their relationship will be discussed in Chapter Seven.

The other two married informants had been separated from their spouses for years. Kurt, now a self-defined loner, had been involved in a brief marriage. He no longer had contact with his wife but as far as he was concerned, he would stay married to her until the day he dies. The lifelong connection Kurt described was not out of love. Kurt explained:

> I've been separated for about three years now. We were married for about three months. It was a good relationship when we first got together. We were together for like six months before we got married. It was a very bad marriage. The courting part of it and the living together was fine, but when it came down to do the marriage license and everything, it just went sour. I was working my ass off, paying rent and buying groceries. I come home and find a black dude in my bed with my old lady. I'm sorry. I don't need to go to bed with somebody that is going to go to bed with somebody else. I just walked in and packed up my duffel bag. I never argued with her or had a confrontation with her. I packed my duffel bag, got in my car, and drove off. That was about three years ago and I haven't been back since.

Kurt had never tried to contact his wife after walking out but he did run into her in a bar about a year later. According to Kurt, she was with a new boyfriend and had never told him she was married. When he walked up to the couple, his wife tried to introduce him as an old friend. Kurt responded:

> I seem to think we have a piece of paper that makes us more than old friends. I'm her husband. If you go talk to her mother you will find out that she is married, she has a marriage license, and she's not divorced. And if she wants a di-

vorce she's going to have to pay for it or you are going to have to pay for it because I'm not. I don't care. I'll stay married till the day I die. I told her she can carry my last name until the day I die. I don't really care. I'm not paying for no divorce. That was the last time I seen her.

The final married informant described a created family unit that was not representative of the sample. Matt, a fifty-two-year-old road dog, was Mormon and claimed to have six spouses. He was married to his first wife in 1968 and according to Matt, she did not care how many wives he had as long as he kept her. At the time of the interview, Matt had not been home in four months because he married his sixth wife without permission from the first five. While the Church of Jesus Christ of Latter-day Saints does not recognize polygamy, Matt claimed his local church did. His church, however, required that permission be secured from all wives before another marriage occurred. His failure to ask his additional wives not only strained his relationships at home but it also resulted in being temporarily barred from his local church. Matt believed that he would be able to return home soon after he was interviewed:

I'll be punished for a while until they get tired of it or they figure they need me. They will drop me a line and tell me it's all right to come home. They will tell me that I can bring her (sixth wife who he also did not live with) home and they will welcome her into the circle. And that is how it is. There's no yelling, no screaming, no arguments, or no fights. Nobody gets a black eye, nobody gets a bloody nose, and nobody gets a dislocated jaw. We sit down and talk about our problems.

Divorce and Death. The divorces described by the informants were certainly less sensational than the marriages. Fifteen (33 percent) respondents, three loners and twelve road dogs, had been divorced. One road dog, Paul, lost his wife to stomach cancer.

There certainly were exceptions to the rule, but the fifteen informants who had experienced marital dissolution described their relationships in a similar fashion. Theme analysis of the interview data revealed five general patterns regarding the way informants practiced intimate relationships. The first consistent theme to surface was the length of most marriages. Most informants' marriages were extremely short. Like Kurt, it was not uncommon for informants to live with their spouse for less than a year. The short duration of the marriages also led to the second theme. Informants who had been married and divorced typically did so more than one time. Many informants had two or three ex-wives in addition to girlfriends with whom they may have had children. The marital experiences of Craig, a thirty-eight-year-old road dog, represent the short nature of many relationships and the propensity towards multiple partners.

I have been married three times. I met a gal while I was in the joint (pen pal). I thought I had to be married so I married her and it didn't last. I didn't live with her for the first four years (while he was in prison). I got out and then I ran into

her. So I moved in with her. That lasted about a month and a half. She was trying to control my life and my health. Her kids were also on my nerves. That
was my third marriage. After four years of being separated I lived under the
same roof for a month and a half.

A few of the informants had marriages that lasted for many years before a
divorce, or in Paul's case, the death of his wife. All of the informants who had
been married for over fifteen years, with the exception of Paul, could be classified as home guards. Home guards are homeless individuals who were not transient but instead lived in one location, most often the city they lived in prior to
becoming homeless. Their connections to the community kept them in the area
even after they ended up on the street. In this study, home guards could be classified either as loners or road dogs depending on their propensity to partner up.
The informants that experienced the dissolution of a long-term marriage repeatedly offered the event as their catalyst to homelessness. Trevor, a fifty-two-year-
old home guard who partnered up, became homeless after his divorce in the late
1980s. Trevor described his married life while simultaneously expressing how
little he was willing to discuss about the subject. "My wife and I moved out to a
farm in 1968. We raised three kids. Got a divorce in 1989. I've been on the
streets ever since. I didn't give a shit after that." Barry, a fifty-four-year-old
home guard and Trevor's road dog, was married for eighteen years. He hit the
streets after his divorce and had little contact with his two boys although his ex-
wife and children lived across town in "his house."

Paul also became homeless after his marriage ended. Before Paul's wife
died he was forced to liquidate all his assets to pay her medical bills. He had
family that were willing to help him out but decided he needed to work through
his grief and get back on his feet financially by himself. He found his situation
very ironic.

> It is kind of funny though. She (wife) was a drug and alcohol counselor so I've
> been around this situation all the time. I've been around the homeless. We did
> volunteer work at all kinds of places. We had people in our house. If she
> couldn't get them in the program right away they would stay for a weekend.
> Then all of the sudden I was on the opposite end of it. Here I am now. You
> know, it could really happen to anybody. I tell you what, most non-alcoholics
> don't realize that they are a few paychecks away. I remember a Charles Kuralt
> program back in the '80s. I think it was called, "You're One Paycheck Away."
> I remember watching it because it was one of the first shows about the home-
> less when we really started realizing that this was a problem in our country.

As represented by Trevor and Barry, the third theme to emerge was that after the divorce informants had little contact with their ex-wives and children.
This led to the fourth pattern of very little support being offered to or received
from the created kin of the informants. These final patterns will be discussed in
the subsequent sections on patterns of exchange.

Based on the descriptions of families of origin a fifth pattern was antici-pated. Because so many of the families of origin were described as abusive, I had anticipated a greater level of violence to be discussed in relation to created kin units. In only a few cases did informants offer even a shred of evidence by stating that their short marriage was "pretty stormy." Informants seldom offered greater detail. John was the exception as he openly discussed his hostility toward his ex-wife in the interview. During one fight with his ex-wife, John, a fifty-three-year-old road dog, put an unloaded shotgun to her head and pulled the trigger just to see if he could scare her. When asked why, he simply claimed that she had "pissed him off." The fact that violence among the informants' created kin was not freely discussed, if it did exist, was not totally surprising because self-incrimination is not a likely occurrence in most interviews.

Fatherhood

Twenty-five (56 percent) of the respondents, five loners and twenty road dogs, were fathers. When asked if they had any children, most of the remaining infor-mants answered, "None that I know of." Of the twenty-five fathers, seventeen had two or more children, many of whom had different mothers.

Despite the high proportion of fathers, few were practicing the role on even a miniscule level. Of the informants with children under eighteen, only one had custody of his child at the time of the interview. Jacob, a thirty-year-old road dog, became housed with his girlfriend and their six-month-old son a couple of weeks before the interview. The rest of the informants' children were raised by their ex-wives or girlfriends, other relatives, or had been placed in foster care. For instance, Craig's children were living in a variety of situations:

> I have four kids ranging from twenty to thirteen. In my immediate family I have a daughter down in Las Vegas. She is thirteen and lives with her mother (second wife). I have one son living with foster parents. I have a daughter liv-ing with her mother, my first wife. And I have a son who is out on his own with a daughter. So I am a grandfather. And that's my kids.

Directly related to the theme that many informants had multiple partners and multiple children was the finding that most children were not planned. Brian, a thirty-year-old road dog, has been tramping for the past six years. When he was twenty-one, he got his girlfriend pregnant. He left when his daughter was about four years old and hadn't seen her since. Brian justified his absence:

> I was just not ready to settle down yet. I mean, I can't really think of it as a mistake because I love my daughter and stuff like that. But it was a mistake in that time in my life because it was not what I wanted to do. I wanted to travel around and stuff like that.

Carter, a fifty-year-old road dog, explained how lucky he had been in that regard. Carter bragged, "I've been with three women in my life and none of them could have kids. Isn't that fantastic."

Overall, for both loner and road dog fathers, the story was quite similar. With the exception of men whose marriages lasted more than a few years, informants who were fathers customarily became so by accident, multiple times, and with multiple women. What they did after conception is the subject of the next section.

Exchanges Between Homeless Men and Their Created Families

The interview data established rates of contact between informants and their created kin that were similar, but less frequent, than contact with families of origin. Road dogs had higher levels of contact and exchange of support but both groups had less than ideal levels. Because many informants had not created many kin units, and had separated from most of those that had been created, there was little contact between informants and created kin. In this section, the frequency of exchanges with created kin will be addressed for both loners and road dogs. Exchanges of support will be separated into intangible and tangible items. As with the discussion of families of creation, the frequency of contact becomes important for assessing intangible exchanges because it is both measurable and informants described emotional connections and exchanges of information as the main reasons for making contact with relatives. Most of the discussion will focus on contact with and support of the informants' children. Like most adults, exchanges with ex-wives or girlfriends were understandably scarce. Contact between fathers and children, however, is typically held to a higher standard.

Intangible Exchanges

Informational and Emotional Exchanges. Informants contacted their created kin for the same basic reasons they kept in touch with their families of origin. Generally, contact was maintained between homeless informants and their created kin because informants felt the need to check in, typically to make sure everything was fine with their children and to let their created kin know they were still alive. The need to maintain at least a minimal level of contact did not generally translate into even sporadic exchanges as it did with some families of origin. Brian, who left his girlfriend and daughter so he could travel, represents the exchange of information on an extremely limited basis. Brian explained: "I've called since then (when he left six years earlier) just to check in to see if she is all right. She's my daughter. I've got to do that. I've probably called twice in the last six years." While Brian's lack of consistent contact with his child was typical of most fathers in the study, separating the discussion between road dogs and loners provides for a better understanding of the family relationships of the informants.

Loners. Throughout this research, a consistent pattern has been revealed. Loners not only lacked many intimate relationships with other homeless individuals and their families of origin, but also with created kin. Of the five loners who were fathers, only one had contact with a child. James, a pool hustler, had five children. He had not had contact with four of his kids in over two years but had a higher level with his youngest son. When James was asked who the most important person in his life was, he replied:

> Well, they say you aren't supposed to have favorites, but I got five children and I would have to say my son, Andy, the youngest one. He is twenty. They all live in town except my daughter. I really don't have much contact with them. They just. . . . They all take after their mother, thank God. She is a school-teacher. She has never drank or done drugs. They (kids) just don't like my life-style. They love me, but they don't want me around. Except for my son Andy. Maybe once every five months I get to see him but he calls me all the time and I call him. He goes to the U (university) down here.

James's comments reveal one of the themes found among informants. It was not uncommon for respondents to have different levels of contact with each of their children. Level of contact typically varied for two reasons. First, as was the case with James, some children were more forgiving than their siblings. Different levels of contact were also found when the informants had children from multiple partners, a common pattern among informants. In these cases the relationship with the ex-wife or girlfriend, as well as their geographic location, contributed to different circumstances and levels of exchange. James was unique in the fact that he kept in contact with his ex-wife. According to James, they talk a couple times a month and she had even asked him to come back to her. James explained the situation:

> I wanted to go back, but I didn't. I was afraid I would hurt her again. They say opposites attract. She didn't drink or smoke and she was educated. I never went back because I knew, me being a street person I got to be out. I am a honky-tonk man I guess. I just know I would hurt her again. There is something that just pulls me. It always has ever since I was a kid.

In three of the five cases, informants desperately wanted more opportunities for exchanging support with their children but were unable. Parker had been homeless since Christmas Day, 1987. On that day he lost his wife and had his two children taken away from him. He tried to call and write his children but his letters were never answered and the phone was always hung up on him. When I asked him to elaborate on his Christmas experience, he only said, "That sucked." Philip, whose children live in Sweden with their mother, also had letters go unanswered and was unable to reach his children by phone. "I'm working so I bought a telephone card and stuff. I try to call over there, but my ex-wife answers the phone and just hangs up. She won't even let me talk to them or nothing." Danny, who referred to himself as a diagnosed loner, met the same obstacles but found an attorney to work *pro bono* in an attempt to secure visitation. In the past three years, Danny had only seen his son a couple of times. Conger, Ge, Elder, Lorenz and Simons (1994) explain that a non-custodial father's relationship with his children is impacted by his relationship with his ex-partner. Since this is a factor within the housed community, it is not a stretch to see this relationship as also a contributing factor among the homeless.

Road Dogs. Road dogs did have higher levels of contact with their children, ex-wives, and girlfriends, but they had nothing about which to brag. There were twenty road dog fathers and only nine had some level of emotional and informational exchanges with at least one child in the last year. Jacob, the exception to the rule, was the only informant that had custody of his child. Trevor had one of the highest levels of contact with his children. Because his children lived in town, he was able to see his son a few times a week, and his two daughters about once a month.

Unlike Trevor, most contact between road dogs and their children was by phone, only allowing for intangible exchanges of support. This finding was also supported for their contact with families of origin. Tommy, now forty-two years old, started using drugs when he was thirteen. During the interview he talked extensively about his seventeen-year-old son that lived in Nevada. He talked to him the day before his interview and did so whenever he could. Tommy explained, "He is 17 years old so it is hard to catch him. I only caught him yesterday as he was on his way out the door to school." When Tommy did not catch his son, he regularly talked with his ex-girlfriend, his son's mother. He let her know what he was doing because, according to Tommy, she probably had more concern for him than anybody did. While Tommy was hitch hiking last summer, he stopped and saw his son and ex-girlfriend for a couple of hours. He did not stay long because, as he explained, "he had to take off."

Eleven of the twenty road dog fathers had lost contact, were not allowed to contact, or had simply walked away from their children. Mark, a forty-four-year-old Vietnam vet, explained how his contact with his ex-wife, his ex-girlfriend, and his children stopped:

> When I married her (first wife) I was sixteen and she was twenty. We had two kids. When she was pregnant again I joined the Marine Corps. I went overseas and spent two tours in Vietnam. The first one was great. The second one I got jacked up (shot). That's why you see me like this (limited use of one leg). When I come back she didn't tell me I wasn't her man anymore, her mother did. She said, "He's not a man anymore." Once my wife learned I was getting

that money (disability), all of the sudden I was a real man. I said get the hell out of my face.

He had not seen his ex-wife or kids since the divorce. Mark's later departure from his long-time girlfriend was also sudden and permanent:

> I lived with her for seven years and we got a little kid. She wanted to get married so bad. I'm not the one to marry her. I said, "Listen to me, I'm not going to marry you, not now. Wait three more years. It will be ten years and you'll know we're going to stick together." I loved her. She loved the hell out of me, but she wouldn't listen. She didn't want to wait ten years. She wanted to get married now. So I said, "Later mama." I took off man. I haven't seen her since. That was 1988.

When he was asked if he had contacted his ex-wife, ex-girlfriend, or his children since leaving them, he stressed: "See, when I drop everything, I drop everything. That's me. When I let go, I let go. I'll never go back to the same woman twice."

Shared Experiences. When road dogs and loners were in contact with their created kin, they described many similar experiences. Many of the common patterns of contact have already been established. Exchanges of support were limited or nonexistent, level of exchange sometimes varied between children, and intangible exchanges typically occurred over the phone. One other theme emerged among the small group of home guards who had some level of contact with children who lived in the area. The common theme for these informants was where they would meet. In most cases, if an informant met their son or daughter instead of calling them, they would do so in a public space rather than at the child's home. According to Trevor:

> They come down here (The Living Room). I just don't feel comfortable going over there (house) because I don't want their friends to see that I'm homeless. I won't embarrass my children. A lot of these guys go out and fly a sign. I couldn't do that. I bet I know two thousand people in the town and they ain't all homeless. I know some bankers, lawyers, doctors, and Indian Chiefs. I've been here a long time.

Tangible Exchanges

Respondents were asked in the interviews if they could count on or would seek support from created family members if they became injured and were no longer able to survive on the street. Informants were also asked about actual support given to and received from their created families. In comparison to families of origin, informants discussed fewer and more limited tangible exchanges with their families of creation.

Financial Aid. Among the informants who had been married or had children, exchange of resources was almost nonexistent. Only a few informants offered support to their created kin, and when they did it typically was financial in nature. Only two of the twenty-five fathers made an attempt to support their children. Walter, a thirty-eight-year-old construction worker, had been homeless for seven years and did his best to support his ex-wife and children in Texas. Walter not only kept in contact with his children, he also regularly sent them money. Walter identified his relationship with his created family:

> I got five kids back in El Paso and that's where I send most of my money. I talk to my kids all the time. But you see four of the kids I raised weren't mine. They're from previous marriages. I knew them since they were little toddlers. I consider them mine. But like I say, I'm just one of those types of people that are kind-hearted. My mama said I had a good heart where I won't turn anybody down and to this day I haven't. If they need my last dollar, I'll give them my last dollar.

While he did send money to his children, he would not consider engaging in a more formal exchange relationship and ask his ex-wife for help if he became injured. According to Walter, she slept with one of his best friends so "that torched just about everything." Danny also had a less than amicable relationship with his child's mother, but continued to send money. Even though Danny's attorney had not been able to secure regular visitation, Danny continued to participate in pharmaceutical trials so he could send his ex-girlfriend money to help support their six year-old son.

Two additional respondents had supported their children in the past, but were no longer able. Lou, a forty-nine-year-old musician, had four children that lived with his parents. According to Lou, "My parents take care of the kids for me. I paid them for it but that account is already closed." Barry, whose ex-wife and kids also lived in town, established funds for his children while he was still married and employed. Barry stated:

> Everybody can call me a bum or whatever. But a lot of people don't know my house is paid for. I got a fund set up for my two kids so when they get out of high school they can go to college. I mean, it is paid for. When I was living at home I would take money and put it into a special account for each kid. When I got divorced in 1986. . . . 1984 or something like that. . . . they had over $6000 in each fund. So by the time they get to college they should have enough to maybe go three years, maybe four. I don't know how much the university costs right now. They should be able to go. It's very important to me. And it is all set up. They have got a place to stay and they're going to have their education. That means a lot to me.

Besides TC, who was married at the time of the interview, informants did not mention the receipt of any financial support from created kin. This was not surprising given the embarrassment factor associated with adult males seeking aid from their created families (Wagner 1993), the nature of most breakups as bitter, and the norm that it is not common to rely on your children for financial assistance. While none of the informant fathers mentioned it as support, the fact that someone else was raising and providing for many of their children was certainly an important form of support.

On the hypothetical level, only a few informants believed they could count on or would even seek support from their ex-wives, girlfriends, or children if their situation worsened. Tommy and James topped this short list. The vast majority of informants would never even consider asking for help from their created kin in such a situation.

Conclusion

This chapter has given attention to a subject previously ignored in the research, the relationships homeless men have with their created kin. The majority of homeless research has focused only on ties to biological kin, homeless families, or group-level street relationships. By including the examination of created kin, the results from this study lay the groundwork for greater examination in future research.

The informants described created families that suffered from even more disruption than their families of origin. Only three of the forty-five respondents were married at the time of the interview and only one of the three was living with his wife. The created families of the informants generally were short-term unions and were commonly formed through accidental conception. Informants also described patterns of multiple wives and girlfriends as well as multiple children.

Contact between homeless informants and created kin was greater for road dogs but both groups had very low levels. Less than half of the twenty-five fathers had contact with their children in the last year. Only a handful of informants had contact with their ex-wives or ex-girlfriends. When contact took place it usually occurred because the informant felt obligated, because they wanted to check in, or because they were offering or seeking support.

Exchange relationships between informants and created kin were almost non-existent. Because support levels were so low for both road dogs and loners, no distinctions could be made between the groups. The only type of support available to a very small number of informants was advice. A few informants were able to rely on created kin to listen to their problems or for advice. As was the case with James and Tommy, such conversations took place with ex-wives and ex-girlfriends with whom they had a child. In the rare cases where more tangible support was offered or received, it was not an equal exchange. Instead of a norm of reciprocity, feelings of family obligations dictated the support.

The data do not portray a strong commitment to created family units among either road dogs or loners. The overall picture showed two distinct paths typically taken by the informants. Roughly half of the informants did not develop created families. The other half created multiple family units but generally failed to ensure their strength and longevity. As with families of origin, the types and levels of exchange relationships with created kin have been covered but further analysis is needed. In the following chapter, explanations for meager levels of exchange between homeless men and their kin will be sought through the lenses of both social exchange and gender theories.

Chapter Six

Can Anyone Exchange a Dime?

Explaining Meager Levels of Exchange

The past two chapters have detailed less than ideal family relationships for the informants. The incidents of family disorganization and other problematic situations accentuated an atmosphere that was not conducive to establishing exchange based relationships. In assessing the themes that surfaced from the data, the depiction of exchange relationships was bleak, but consistent. These men reported scarce contact and engaged in only minimal, if any, relationships of exchange with their families of origin and creation. In attempting to explain the meager levels of exchange, two theoretical avenues were pursued. The relationships between homeless men and their families were examined through the lenses of both gender and social exchange theory. Both theories were highlighted by the informants' perspectives in order to explain the relationships documented between informants and their families of origin and creation.

Because the themes derived from the data regarding respondents' explanations for a lack of contact with and support from families of origin and creation were similar for loners and road dogs, they will be discussed together. In examining the meager levels of exchange, theoretical lenses that connected the themes of the interviews with the social and economic constraints faced by the informants were needed. To achieve this goal, two theories, gender theory and social exchange theory, were used to provide a greater opportunity for expanding upon the explanation offered by informants as to why most were isolated from their families of origin and creation.

Gender Theory

Gender theory is a useful tool in explaining the constraints placed on men's and women's behavior in the public and private spheres of work and home. With this theoretical lens, men's actions toward their families of origin and creation were not seen as the separate and isolated acts of individuals, but patterns of gendered behavior. As Risman (1998) and Martin (2003) both explain, gender is a structure that includes expected patterns of behavior which work to constrain individuals. The constraints, and corresponding liberties, of the family-based behaviors of the homeless men were the focus of this examination. One of the most pervasive themes derived from the data was that being a man dictated a great deal of their actions on the street and in relation to their family. This is not unique to homeless men. Gender theory is valuable because it provides a benchmark for the level of contact and exchange housed men have with their nonresident families of origin and creation, providing a basis for analysis when examining the actions of informants.

Families of Origin

In general, there is some expectation that adults maintain contact with their nonresident families. However, exchange-based relationships, especially those involving adult males, are not extremely common. Lawton, Silverstein, and Bengtson (1994) estimate almost 70 percent of adult children have some type of contact with their mothers on a weekly basis. Lye, Klepinger, Hyle, and Nelson (1995) contend that over one-third of adults have face-to-face contact with their parents at least once a week. Exchange relationships between adults and nonresident family members are less common with only one-quarter of adult children indicating that they give or receive advice and emotional support with their parents (Eggebeen and Hogan, 1990). When examining such family exchanges, gender tends to play an important role. In studies of middle-aged adults, Lee, Spitze, and Logan (2003), Shuey and Hardy (2003), and Rosenthal (1985) all concluded that daughters were much more likely to play the role of kin keeper with parents. In an assessment of the support among homeless and poor individuals, Bares and Toro (1999) concluded that women reported higher levels of support and larger family networks than men.

As indicated by previous research, the bar has not been set terribly high as to the level of exchange adult men are expected to engage in with family members. From a gender perspective, this is important given that a common expectation of gender-based behavior is that middle-aged men do not need to be cared for and the care of elderly parents or in-laws is more often left to women (Abel 1991). The idea that adult men should be independent and should be responsible for their own well-being (Aldous 1995) resonated with the study informants. Informants repeatedly commented that they refused to seek help from their family members because they were adults and could fend for themselves. Kurt, who lived in his van, concluded: "I'm forty-three years old. I'm a big man. I'm old enough to stand on my own two feet and take care of myself. If I get down and stuck out on the street, then that's my problem. I'm not a little kid. They don't have to babysit me." This sentiment was especially common when informants were asked about seeking support from their created families. When Trevor was asked if he had sought assistance from his ex-wife or three children, he responded:

> I'm a firm believer in the Constitution of the United States. One of the functions of government is to care for each and every individual in this damn country. I don't care who you are. I earned that right to have medical care (through military service). So why would I burden my family or friends when there's no reason for it?

Family members' other obligations were also mentioned on several occasions as a reason for limited contact and requests for support. Although Randy cited his sister's distaste for his lifestyle as the reason why she would not help him, besides cigarettes and five dollars at Thanksgiving, he also revealed that he would never ask for help. He would never turn to his sister because she was trying to raise her own family and her husband is dying of cancer. According to Randy, "She's got enough headaches to have to try to help out her older brother." Clearly, Randy's position as the older male sibling played a part in his unwillingness to ask his sister for help.

Randy's comments also reflected another theme regarding the way gendered expectations play a role in sibling support. Lee, Mancini, and Mexwell (1990) related that sisters were more likely than brothers to provide support to family members. In this study, bonds between sisters also appeared to be stronger than ties between brothers or opposite sex siblings. In only two of the interviews did the informant mention regular contact with a brother. In one case, the informant would occasionally send his imprisoned brother letters and extra money. The only other case was Craig showing up drunk at his brother's house in the middle of the night just to say, "Hey bro, what's happening?" In short, data from this study indicate that brothers were not utilized, or even considered as potential exchange partners. Further evidence of the value of gender theory is derived from the finding that more men in the study contacted their mothers than any other relative.

As explained in Chapter Four, emotional and informational exchanges were more likely to take place with mothers than with any family or origin or creation. As Craig stated earlier, the pressure to be honest with his mom led him to reveal more than he planned. Mothers were also seen as a good source of advice and information for the informants. Typically, informants contacted their mothers and all the family information was disseminated through her. After getting the scoop on what their fathers and siblings were doing, if they existed, many informants did not feel the need to contact any other relative. Don, who used to live with his mother before becoming homeless, also believed this was the case:

> Generally whenever I talk to Mom I find out how everyone is doing. Once in a while I call my sister but she doesn't like it if I call collect. Mom doesn't mind. Most guys on the street talk about this. What I hear mostly is like they may not talk to their brothers or sisters, but they always stay in touch with their mother. If they still have a father a lot of guys get into conflict with their father so they

may not be in touch with them. The mothers, no matter what, they are usually there.

Obviously the level of reported contact, as measured through surveys and interviews, suggests that many informants did not have any contact with their mothers. However, when there was contact with a family member, it was likely to be with their mom. This finding was consistent with earlier research on the housed community. Silverstein and Bengtson (1997), as well as Lawton et al. (1994), concluded that intergenerational solidarity was stronger between mothers and their children than the bonds expressed between fathers and their adult children. Using the lens of gender theory, mothers, not adult sons, were seen as kin keepers.

Families of Creation

Gender theory was especially applicable in examining the freedom men are afforded within their families of creation. Within families of creation, men and women are seen as having different responsibilities. Men are seen as the traditional breadwinners and women as the nurturers. The assignment of such roles is neither natural nor traditional according to the gender perspective (Ferree 1990). Such notions stem from the shift to an industrialized economy (Glass 2000; Ferree 1990; Pleck 1987) when work was separated from the home for the first time in history as well as men's greater ability to flex economic power. Despite its relatively recent origin, and even research that shows greater blending of duties in the home (Deutsch and Saxon 1998), such belief systems work toward the advantage of men's freedoms. Within contemporary marriages, men's breadwinner label continues to provide greater financial power and justifies a general lack of childcare participation (Townsend 2002).

The majority of men in the study, however, were neither married nor served as breadwinners for their families. Their family position, or lack thereof, provided them with little obvious power to exert. This did not mean that gender theory was inapplicable. In fact, examining relationships that have ended through divorce or separation provides a significant opportunity to view the structure of gender in operation. For example, given that the overwhelming majority of women have custody after a separation (Eggebeen, Snyder, and Manning 1996), the expectations for custodial parenting among fathers is low. Warshak (1996) explains that women maintaining primary responsibility for their children following a divorce is simply a continuation of their gendered responsibilities from the marriage. Men, on the other hand, are defined more through the provider role. When they no longer live under the same roof with those they are supposed to be providing for, connections between family members can be strained or lost. According to Stephens (1996), Seltzer (1991), and others, contact between non-custodial fathers and children tends to diminish quickly and dramatically for the majority of children.

Gender theory provides at least partial explanations for why many fathers in the study severely limited, or stopped outright, their contact with and support of their children. West and Zimmerman (1987) coined the term "doing gender" to explain how individuals acquire their gender identity and express it to those around them. For many fathers, doing gender is often reflected in breadwinning activities. Following a relationship breakup, this connection is often challenged and frequently severed. According to Catlett and McKenry (2004), non-custodial fathers frequently cite the loss of respect and authority when dealing with their children, both important aspects of the identity and definition of fatherhood. Furstenberg and Cherlin (1991) explain that the gendered division of labor that was part of the relationship is lost following a divorce or separation, which often leads to an eventual withdrawal of support from the family. This may happen, according to Catlett and McKenry (2004), because divorce strips men's position of relative privilege and negatively impacts their construction of masculinity. The connection between masculinity and breadwinning is problematic on many levels, including the way such ideas impact relationships with partners and children. For the informants, the connection became especially problematic because they were not able to fulfill their role as provider. A number of studies have examined the negative consequences for men following divorce, such as loss of social relationships with friends and family, loss of a home, loss of identifying roles, and problems with emotional and physical health (i.e., Catlett and McKenry 2004; Kiecolt-Glaser and Newton 2001; Braver 1998; Kruk 1994). While this study cannot make a direct link between divorce and the current state of homelessness for informants, such problems were the everyday realities of the men in the study.

Despite the evidence among the housed community suggesting that non-resident fathers are seeing their children more (Amato and Gilbreth 1999), informants did not appear to be following that trend. Informants did not use the same words, but several indicated that because they had started new lives they could not keep contacting and supporting their created kin. What this typically meant was that they had abandoned their responsibilities for their children. Among the informants, only two of the non-custodial fathers even attempted to support their children. As previously reported, after leaving his girlfriend of seven years and his children, Mark explained, "See, when I drop everything, I drop everything. That's me." Craig had four children and had been married three times at the time of the study. When he divorced his second wife, the following situation was created:

I was married to her about three years. When we split she got a son out of the deal and I got a son. And about the time we split she was pregnant so she got a daughter out of the deal too. My son (under his custody) is now in a foster-type setting. It is not state foster care. It is more of a private situation. He is doing better. This guy is a pretty responsible dude. He had a couple of older daughters that moved away from home and he has probably always wanted a son so he has kind of taken over mine. And my son is doing good in school. He ain't got his old man. I pretty much dropped responsibilities. I wasn't responsible for anything anymore.

The ability to drop responsibilities with little familial or societal consequence is freedom unavailable to women. Gender theory speaks directly to this. Women instead are bound by the "tender-years presumption" that assumes that women are better fit for raising children, especially the very young (Warshak 1996). While gender theorists (i.e., Ferree 1990; Pleck 1987) point out that parenting and breadwinning differences are not innate, or even traditional, the myth of natural differences remains strong. The belief that mothers are naturally more capable as parents (Silverstein 1996) provides for a gendered idea of parenting, both custodial and non-custodial, that is more forgiving to men who shirk their duties. Within the model of gender theory, gender is seen as a lifelong process of behaviors that reflect and reproduce the material and ideological advantages men hold (Ferree 1990). As such, the finding that most men in the study walked away from their relationships can be explained by a loss of the provider role and the resulting loss of masculinity, but it can also be examined as an exertion of power. Some of the informants appeared to take advantage of these gendered expectations, while others were victims of a narrow definition of fathering based on the role as provider.

Social Exchange Theory

Through the discussion of gender theory, it was established that adult children, especially men, do not typically engage in exchange relationships with their families of origin (Hogan, Eggebeen and Clogg 1993) and post-divorce contact between children and non-custodial fathers is less than ideal (Amato and Gilbreth 1999; Furstenberg and Cherlin 1991). The picture, however, is not complete. The inclusion of social exchange theory provides a more comprehensive explanation as to why homeless men do not engage in frequent exchange relationships. Thematic analysis of the interview and survey data revealed several themes offered by the informants as to what constituted exchange relationships and why they were so rare. Such themes included limited resources, burnt bridges, bridges that were never constructed, and geographic proximity.

Limited Resources

The themes of unemployment and a lack of intergenerational support found in previous research were themes that also rang true for informants. In fact, such realities also applied to many of the men's housed families of origin and creation. In short, having limited financial resources was a major reason offered by many informants as to why they did not support any created kin or members of their family of origin. They quite simply could not provide their family members with something they themselves did not possess. Not surprisingly, this is a consistent conclusion in the research. For example, Hogan et al. (1993) found living in poverty reduces the likelihood an individual will give support or receive intergenerational family support. In examining post-divorce contact between noncustodial fathers and children, Bradshaw, Stimson, Skinner, and Williams (1999) reported that employed fathers were twice as likely to have regular contact with their children as were men who were unemployed.

Among informants, the inability to offer support became a greater problem because it was linked to their willingness to be in contact with family, thus limiting further possibilities for even intangible exchange-based relationships. The inability to provide support was typically offered as a justification for not contacting their created kin. Some informants did not want to have any contact with created family members because it served as a reminder that they were destitute. Wagner (1993) contends that even when there are not burnt bridges between family members, which will be discussed in the following section, many homeless will not make contact because they are embarrassed. The embarrassment, according to Wagner (1993), stems not only from their situation, but also because they do not have the ability to form a reciprocal relationship.

While it may seem obvious that the homeless informants had little to exchange, they were often not alone in their poverty. Housed families of the informants, both created and those of origin, were also frequently unable to engage in numerous financial exchanges. The majority of the respondents described the financial situations during their childhood as quite tenuous. Because the majority of informants came from families that were financially strapped, it was no surprise then that many of the informants refused to ask for help, and sometimes even refused to initiate contact given the limited means of their families. Terrance, at forty-six years of age, still called his mother the most important person in his life, but refused to ask her for any more help. He explained that his mother and stepfather were barely making it through life, so although they would help him, he wouldn't ask for it. Terrance's refusal to ask and his parents' perceived inability to help demonstrate the strength of drawing from both gender and social exchange theories.

Burnt Bridges

Beyond family poverty, informants frequently stated that they could not establish exchange-based relationships with members of their family because they had burned too many bridges. The burning of relationship bridges with both families of origin and creation was the most consistent theme to surface through the interview data. Bridges ultimately became burned for four general reasons including family members having issues with respondent's lifestyles, hostile breakups with created family members, simply having asked for assistance too often, and having some family members serve as gatekeepers to other kin.

The first reason included arguments over drugs, alcohol, or other behaviors. Although the exact percentages are hotly disputed, as well as issues of cause or consequence, conservative estimates conclude that between one-fourth and one-third of homeless abuse alcohol, drugs, or both (Tessler and Dennis 1992). When homeless drug users were interviewed, Sterk-Elifson and Elifson (1992) discovered that around one-third of their sample mentioned that at one time they received more support from their relatives. The support available to those persons decreased as their drug habit increased. Among homeless youth, recent studies have also found extremely high rates of drug use. For example, both Bousman et al. (2005) and Whitbeck and Hoyt (1999) found up to 80 percent of youth in their research had used drugs and or alcohol in the three months to one year prior to the study. Substance abuse was a problem with at least 40 percent of the study participants. For instance, before he became homeless, Kent's mother and stepfather used to support him. The support stopped when he started using drugs in his teens. At the time of the interview, his mother and stepfather did not want him coming home for any more than a short visit. According to Kent, "I can visit and everything like that but they don't want drugs in their home. I agree with them. I need to get my shit together. They used to support me with money for things like music and cigarettes and stuff like that, but I ended up using it on drugs. Now I am on the street. It was a wrong move."

According to Eric, his alcoholism has had a negative impact on his relationships with his children. He had never been married but had three children with three different women. He described his contact with his children:

> My first daughter, I've only seen her once for about three seconds. My son is in foster care because his mom is a crack addict. My other daughter I just seen her not too long ago. I took her out and spent about three grand on her for Christmas. After that her mom filed a restraining order against me. All kinds of lies and shit saying I beat my daughter and stuff like that because I showed up there drunk. I got a drinking problem. I'm an alcoholic. I showed up there and started threatening her one night so I kind of burnt that bridge. I figured when my daughter is old enough to make her own decisions she'll decide if she wants to see me.

Many of the homeless men in the sample who used drugs and alcohol expressed their family's perspective that any support would reward their behavior. Cameron, now forty-one years old, had been a chronic alcoholic since the age of fifteen. In 1976, he was sent to prison on charges related to drinking. This event caused his family to disown him. Cameron claimed that as long as he is an alcoholic, his mother and siblings refuse to have anything to do with him.

It should be noted that though rare, burnt bridges like Cameron's were sometimes reparable. Cleve, a forty-year-old alcoholic road dog, was not able to get help from his family for years. According to Cleve, for three years he was "out on a limb and couldn't stand up straight because of his drinking." Since he had stopped drinking, he had increased contact with his brothers and sisters and could now count on them for at least limited support.

Disapproval over behavior, and the resulting lack of contact and support, can work both ways. For example, Jason came from a family of alcoholics and because of his background refused to be around anyone, including family members, who had been drinking. Jason explained:

> My mom died. She was an alcoholic. She drank herself to death pretty much. She died at thirty-eight back in 1980 or '81. All (relatives) on her side are alcoholics in California. My brother is an alcoholic. My uncle and cousins, they are all alcoholics. I really shy away from any kind of. . . . I can't be around somebody that's drunk, so I don't get along with them very well. They're not very close to me.

Disagreements over general philosophies of work and life could also burn bridges between informants and their housed families. Randy, a road dog in his forties, did not know his father, and his mother died a few years earlier. He had a sister but she was unwilling to help him because, according to Randy, "My sister doesn't like the fact that I worry about me instead of anybody else." Randy had an ex-wife and children that he did not contact or support.

Marty also had lost his mother and was unable to rely on his sister. After Marty's mother died when he was fifteen, he moved in with his older sister. Marty's sister had two children of her own and according to Marty was not supportive or loving towards him. Marty moved out after six months and was placed in foster care. When he turned eighteen, he began staying with a number of friends until he landed in a Salvation Army shelter. Marty elaborated why he moved out of his sister's home and how he thought his sister would react if he would tell her he was homeless:

> The money was what she talked about from the day I moved in. I had to find my own ride to and from work. She lived in a small town and the nearest town I was able to get work was eleven miles away. So for me to get a ride to and from work was a little difficult since I was only fifteen. The love was real hard pressed. She's got two little boys and now she's got a teenager dumped on her. So that was kind of a burden on the family. Plus, I'm not a Christian. I was raised with Christian values, but I haven't found my God in the Bible. You know, I've been to mass, to synagogues, to all the different things. I believe there is something greater than myself, but I haven't found it written down yet. Well, my sister teaches Sunday school. You can see where that one was going. If I went to her and said, look, I'm homeless, she would say, "Well, go to the Church on Wednesdays, they have soup and salad." That is kind of how my family is. So I've learned to depend more on my friends than I ever have on my family.

The second theme that surfaced was that bridges were commonly burned between informants and their created families as a result of bad breakups. Bitter breakups occurred for a variety of reasons but the end result was the same in that contact and support with created kin almost always ceased immediately. Cameron described the situation after breaking up with his girlfriend:

I had another girlfriend and she saw me with her so that stirred up the fire even more. She told me she was going to go home and tell the kids that I had died so I shouldn't bother coming back around. And if I did come back around, she was even going to make it real difficult for me. She said she would even go as far as paying somebody to kill me. I would like to see my kids, but I don't want to be around her.

Within the housed community, Conger et al. (1994) found that a man's relationship with his ex-spouse may negatively influence the quality of his relationship with his children. Given the themes of addictions, infidelity, abandonment, etc. that surfaced as informants described the breakups, it was not surprising that few fathers had contact with their children. This was definitely the case with John, a fifty-three-year-old road dog, who described one of his last conversations with his ex-wife:

I had just got out of jail. I had been in jail for second-degree murder because this guy pissed me off. When I was in jail they brought me the papers. She wanted me to pay child support and alimony. I called her and told her that it was not funny. I told her if she ever did it again then I would have to go up there and shoot her. I got away with this one (He was released from jail because his second-degree murder charges were dropped) and I will have to come up there and kill you.

The third reason offered by informants as to why bridges were burnt was because they had already asked for too much. In many cases, such as Kent, informants mentioned that they used to receive help but family members tired of the request. Family members typically refused to offer additional support when they did not think the money or other support was being used wisely or because it did not appear to be doing any good. In such cases the informants generally did not have a confrontation with their relatives, it was simply clear that they had worn out their welcome. When Craig, who by thirty-eight had already had five heart attacks, was asked if he would seek help from his family if he had another heart attack, he concluded:

No, I don't think I would. There are other agencies. They have given me help in the past and I think I have probably worn that out with my lifestyle. There are agencies for that. If things get tough I turn myself in for a thirty day treatment. If I am freezing on the street I can go to the Salvation Army. If I can't get into a program I can go there and tell them I feel like killing myself or I will harm somebody else. Then I will be in the nut hut for however much time. There are other places and means to getting help other than family.

As expressed by Craig, not relying on family did not mean everything had to be accomplished alone. In addition to relying on friends, the subject of Chapter Seven, government and nonprofit agencies, were included in the limited arsenal of support for the men. The importance of agencies, and more importantly, the workers and volunteers representing the agency, were found to be very important in a number of studies on homeless youth and adults (i.e., Kurtz et al. 2000; Fischer and Breakey 1991). As Craig revealed, these "dodges" could be used instead of relying on the grace of family members.

The final theme offered by informants as to why bridges had burned could be in reaction to any of the first three reasons. It was not uncommon for a parent or child of an informant to want to have more contact or offer more support but they were blocked, or at least discouraged, from doing so by other family members. The protesting family members often objected to support or contact with their homeless relative because of past confrontations or feelings that the informants were taking advantage of their kin. Peter would like to see his father, who he considered the most important person in his life, but his mother was standing in the way. Peter was a thirty-one-year-old loner and was sleeping in front of The Living Room at the time of the interview. When asked if he could count on his parents for aid if his situation drastically worsened, he replied, "My dad would, but my mom would put her foot down. She would never let that happen again." When asked what caused a falling out between him and his mother, Peter frankly replied, "Her mouth."

Don also met with resistance when he accepted help from his mother. He used to live with his mother in Kansas City but his siblings put a great deal of pressure on him to move out. Don had been homeless before moving back with his mother, but his brothers and sisters thought he was taking advantage of their mom. Don, on the other hand, believed that he was helping her because he was paying half the rent and utilities, something his siblings were not doing. Eventually, Don did move out and left Kansas City.

Bridges Never Built

Identifying the shared experiences informants offered as to why they did not have more contact and opportunities for exchange with their families revealed the theme that many informants were never able to build bridges with their families. For many of these men, the reasons they gave for the lack of support stemmed back to the quality of their family relationships. Incidents of family disorganization created situations for most informants where they were unable or refused to contact family members.

Of the forty-five informants, twenty-eight (62 percent) experienced the death of at least one parent or stepparent, and nine (20 percent) spent a considerable amount of time raised in foster homes, orphanages, group homes, or with relatives other than their parents. Almost all of the respondents described families of origin that had serious disruptions and problems. In other cases, informants did not even have alternative family arrangements. Instead, they had to fend for themselves. As described in Chapter Four, Eric began living on his own when he was fourteen years old and Jason, while housed, received little if any attention from his father. As argued by Whitbeck, Hoyt, and Huck (1994), adult childrens' support roles are influenced by emotional attachments established earlier in the relationship, an area seriously lacking among informants.

Another way bridges were never built was quite common among the informants and their children. Given the findings regarding bad breakups, multiple created families, and short unions, it was not surprising that many informants were not allowed or chose not to form relationships with their children. Informants repeatedly mentioned that their created families had "moved on" as a reason why contact and support were limited or non-existent. Don commented on what he typically saw with his homeless friends:

> You have guys that try and stay in touch with their children and with their ex-wife. Then sometimes the woman will get remarried. Then the new husband really doesn't appreciate them (father/ex-husband) being there. My friend got a divorce and he tried to stay in touch with the kids but the kids' stepfather didn't want him around. There wasn't a court order or anything, but the new husband didn't trust him. Every time they got together they got into a fight.

Ricky, a 33 year-old addict, detailed a similar situation:

> I was in a program getting myself together. My roommate kept telling me about this girl. I became friends with her and a couple months later we ended up sleeping together. We stayed friends for a year or so and then she got pregnant. I moved in with her for a while. That didn't work out too well so I went back to the Salvation Army. We stayed in contact though. The time came when she went to the hospital to have her baby and there's two men walking the aisle waiting on this baby. I asked the other guy if he was having a baby. He said, "Yea, my wife is." I asked him who his wife was and he said, "Samantha." I said, "That's my baby." And he said, "Well, that's my wife." I got to spend some time with my child but they ended up packing everything up and heading to Michigan. I haven't seen or heard of her for like four years.

The discussion of burnt bridges revealed that some situations were even more complicated and potentially harmful, such as Cameron's ex-wife threatening to have him killed if he ever came to see the children. Bradshaw et al. (1999) found that the most common reason reported by non-custodial fathers in their study for their lack of contact was that their ex-partners had blocked their access. Given that it is difficult to get accurate measures of both sides of the story in such studies, the research on the extent and effectiveness of gate-keeping between custodial and non-custodial parents is not definitive (Dunn 2004). The academic arguments, however, meant little to informants like Cameron.

Geographic Distance

Among the housed community, Horwitz (1993), as well as Spitze and Logan (1991), reported that greater physical distance between adult children and parents is associated with less contact and weaker feelings of obligation. Among the homeless, barriers of distance and limited transportation options become magnified.

The general mobility of homeless men serves as yet another obstacle to forming exchange-based relationships with housed family members. Given that only six (13 percent) of the respondents were home guards, the majority of the sample were more transient in their lifestyle. Attempting to determine how far each respondent was from their closest family members was undertaken after the interviews were completed, so only rough estimates were available. The decision was made to attempt to estimate the distance between Plainview, where the interviews took place, and their parent's home. The home of informants' parents was chosen as the default reference point given the finding that informants were more likely to have contact and engage in exchanges with mothers than any other family member. If the informants' parents were not alive, or it was clear they had no contact with them, distance was estimated between Plainview and the family member of origin or creation with whom the respondent had the most contact. In four cases (9 percent), informants had not had any contact with any family member in the past few years and were removed from the estimate. Given these restrictions, the estimated mean distance between respondents interviewed in Plainview, home guards included, was approximately seven hundred miles. A distance of seven hundred miles, or even one hundred miles for that matter, is a severe impediment to maintaining exchange relationships. As Snow and Mulcahy (2001) explained, the homeless by definition are spatially and residentially marginalized. By comparison, Lawton et al. (1994) estimate that over half of adult children live within an hour's drive of their parents.

Conclusion

This study has given attention to a subject previously ignored in the research by examining the level of contact and exchange negotiated between homeless men and their families of origin and creation. The results indicate that the majority of the informants lacked consistent family contact and were even less likely to engage in exchange relationships. For example, 47 percent of respondents had no contact with any members of their family of origin in the year prior to the interview and only ten of the twenty-five fathers had any contact with their children in the past year. Not surprisingly, contacts with ex-wives and ex-girlfriends were almost non-existent. When contact was made with family members, it typically involved short phone calls to exchange information, and possibly to make an emotional connection, but rarely involved more than brief visits. When measuring levels of exchange, only meager exchanges were made between the informants and their families of origin and even fewer were engaged in with their families of creation. For instance, only eleven respondents received any financial assistance from their families of origin and only two of the twenty-five fathers had made any attempt to financially support their children in the past year. Besides exchanges of information, the most direct examples of exchange-based relationships were demonstrated when sons participated in household maintenance tasks in exchange for temporary shelter.

Drawing from social exchange theory allowed the focus to include the structural constraints placed on these men. Despite Rubin's (1985) contention that family members can usually be counted on for assistance even when no pattern of exchange has previously existed, the men in the study had little support to draw from. Informants described families with little resources and relationships with families that did not welcome exchanges of resources.

Gender theory also helped to establish a baseline for comparison of exchanges taking place between nonresident family members in the housed community. Hogan et al. (1993) estimated that half of Americans do not participate in exchange relationships with their parents. The baseline for comparison becomes even lower when gender is taken into account. In short, it became clear that even among the housed community, adult men are not expected to play a major role in kin keeping (Furstenberg and Cherlin, 1991). Gender differences can even be found after a couple with children breaks up, as was the case with twenty-five informants. According to Silverstein and Bengston (1997), post-divorce non-custodial mothers have stronger relationships with their children than do non-custodial fathers. Gender theory helped to explain the lack of contact and support with created families through an examination of the men's loss of their gendered identity as a provider as well as their greater leeway when stepping away from the situation.

The inclusion of both gender and social exchange theories highlighted the perspectives offered by informants as to the state of their family relationships. Informants noted that they had limited resources, lived long distances from their families, had burnt several relationship bridges, experienced family disorganization, and had a general unwillingness to seek or provide support. Given these roadblocks to the maintenance of family relationships, it is not surprising that contact and exchanges were limited. For example, one might not expect a great deal of opportunity for exchange to take place given the average distance between informants and family members was seven hundred miles. It is also not surprising that when exchanges did occur, transfers of information and emotional support were the most common forms of exchange. Drawing from the informants' perspective, social exchange theory, and gender theory all contributed to greater understanding of why these men did not maintain strong family relationships.

Chapter Seven

I Got Me a Road Dog

Virginia, a former director of The Living Room, portrayed the situation of many homeless as "hopeless" because they had nowhere to turn. In describing those who frequented the shelter, Virginia explained, "These people have no connections. These people have no significant relationships. And I have been saying that for a long time. They may have family but for whatever reason they are not seen as major sources of support, either emotional or economic."

Despite Virginia's bleak outlook, and study findings reaffirming the lack of support from families of origin and creation, the homeless have alternative sources of support. One strategy to deal with the loss of affiliation from families of origin and creation was to affiliate with people who are in the same predicament. Relying on other homeless, however, does not mean that all relationships of this type are the same. For example, Dordick (1997) explored four distinct groups of homeless in New York City and found group level relationships, heterosexual ties, homosexual ties, and men who remained rather isolated despite residing in the same small shelter. McCarthy et al. (2002), Pollio (1994), Sterk-Elifson and Elifson (1992), Snow and Anderson (1993), La Gory et al. (1991), Baumann and Grisby (1988), Mitchell (1987), and a host of others have also documented street relationships. Because the majority of past studies have focused on short-term arrangements and group-level cooperation, such relationships have been described as fragile and far from intimate. All relationships that form between homeless men do not fit that description. What the literature lacks is an examination of the long-term, non-sexual partnerships formed between two homeless men. The following discussion takes a step toward filling that void by detailing road dog relationships among homeless men.

Being, or having, a road dog did not have the same meaning to every informant. Road dog relationships were described by some as very superficial and short-lived while others expressed that they could last years and become very intimate partnerships. Partnership length and the use of familial terms to describe partners were used to distinguish lifelong road dogs from road dogs only partnering up for the duration of a particular journey. To bring to light these relationships, new action and social exchange theories were employed. Exchange theory was necessary to explain why road dogs formed relationships in the first place. It is argued that street partnerships began simply as exchange-based relationships helpful for survival. Most road dogs in the study never progressed beyond this stage. The exceptions to this rule, however, could not be fully explained through social exchange theory. In cases where road dogs moved beyond basic exchange relationships and began to think of themselves as family members, new action theory was employed. New action theory was used to conceptualize the construction of primary groups in response to an individual's lack of resources and traditional family ties. Through the lens of new action theory, a justification for referring to lifelong road dogs as fictive kin will be offered. However, the argument will not be presented that lifelong road dogs remained in such relationships as fictive kin for extremely long periods. Even the most intimate and stable road dogs eventually parted company and explanations for why these relationships ended will be given.

Generalized Exchanges

Options for support on the street were not limited to housed family members, social service agencies, or committing to a street partner. Both road dogs and loners were able to draw support from a more general, yet important, source. Interactions between homeless individuals are often governed by a general feeling or philosophy that you should do unto others as you would have them do unto you. This philosophy of life on the street was carried out by being helpful to those who were in the same situation you were in without the expectation of reciprocity. For example, giving your last dollar, cigarette, or coat to a stranger with the expectation that it would not be returned and nothing would be offered in exchange was quite common. Ricky, who was sleeping outside of The Living Room with a group of men and women, explained that even though someone on the streets may only have one dollar left because it had been three days since they donated plasma, they would still give it to someone who needed it. They simply knew, according to Ricky, that a dollar, a blanket or a cigarette would come back to them from someone else, "because it is out of their hearts." According to Uehara (1990), Scanzoni and Marsiglio (1993), and others, such indirect exchanges are an example of one of the two components of dual exchange theory, generalized exchange.

In brief, social exchange theory describes decisions to form, maintain, and dissolve relationships as basically a conscious balance of advantages and disadvantages (Blau 1964; Homans 1961; Thibaut and Kelly 1959). More recent interpretations of social exchange theory have distinguished between two separate types of exchange. Uehara (1990) borrows from Ekeh's (1974) dual exchange theory to explain that social exchanges can either be generalized or restricted in nature. Restricted exchanges closely resemble the elementary exchanges described in the earlier works on social exchange theory (i.e., Homans 1961). Restricted exchanges usually take place between two actors and reciprocity is almost always expected (Ekeh 1974). This component of dual exchange will be discussed in the following section on road dogs.

Providing general assistance to an individual based on the idea that someone else in the group or community will in turn offer a kind gesture fits into the category of generalized exchanges. Generalized exchange is based on the principle of indirect reciprocity and typically takes place among groups (Uehara 1990) such as Ricky's companions outside of The Living Room. Several examples of generalized exchanges can be found in the research on economically disadvantaged blacks (i.e., Uehara 1990; Jewell 1988; Gerstel and Gross 1987; Stack 1974; Liebow 1967) and the homeless (Kurtz et al. 2000; Dordick 1997; Snow and Anderson 1993; Rivlin and Imbimbo 1989). Examples of generalized exchanges were also easily revealed in the present study. When discussing why many homeless looked out for each other, Paul, who used to volunteer at homeless shelters before his wife died and he ultimately became homeless himself, concluded:

> It is a close knit group out here because society looks down on us. Lots of people look at us and say, "he's a homeless bum." So they've developed a little culture. They know they can't call on society for help. We work our own problems out. Screw you! We don't need their shit! The homeless become close because one guy can say, "You need a winter coat don't you? You can go about fourteen blocks over there and they will get you a good deal on a coat." Just like Ryan, a guy that comes in here all the time. Ryan has had three coats this year and he has given them all away because he found guys that needed a coat more. They (the homeless) got their own culture because everybody looks down their noses at them. They are going to keep doing it because if they don't keep passing the word to help each other, people out here (housed society/government) are just going to trample all over them. They really are you know.

Acts of generalized exchange were also explained by many informants as merely the right thing to do. While detailing his willingness to help strangers, Jerry, a thirty-eight-year-old road dog proudly revealed, "That's where the old saying comes from. 'Jerry has helped more tramps than God.'" Ricky, who gave a stranger one of his blankets two nights before the interview, expressed, "I got morals. It makes me feel good to be able to help somebody and I think we're all like that. You know we are out in the middle of the cold and no one likes to see somebody else freezing."

Feelings of Solidarity

According to Uehara (1990), patterns of generalized exchange often lead to feelings of solidarity among its participants. This was evident when informants were asked to describe the social atmosphere of The Living Room. Road dogs, as well as loners, commonly expressed feelings of solidarity as they talked about the men and women who also frequented The Living Room. For example, Stan, a thirty-seven-year-old road dog and lifelong resident of Plainview, revealed:

> The Living Room to me is like vocational rehab. It's the best in the world because you're making friends, lifetime friends. You'll never look at another homeless person as homeless. You feel like you're part of a brotherhood. Like maybe somebody who went to a fraternity or a lodge or something. . . . even more than that. Like somebody who you were in a combat zone with. You feel camaraderie towards a lot of these people. There are people I would give my last dollar to, my last cigarette, or my meal, because I know they would do it to me.

As demonstrated by Stan, feelings of solidarity may not only be a reflection of generalized exchange but also of shared experiences. The fact that each homeless person knew what hardships their counterparts were going through, and that they are willing to share their last dollar with an acquaintance, or even a stranger, likely produced a sense of solidarity among those frequenting The Living Room.

A small number of homeless studies not only cite feelings of solidarity, but also the creation of group-level fictive kinship networks based almost solely on generalized exchanges (Wagner 1993; Rivlin and Imbimbo 1989). Fictive kinship networks based on generalized exchanges were not found in this study. Feelings of solidarity and commitment, however, were repeatedly expressed in family terms. For example, when the comment was made to Ricky that he seemed to know almost everyone at The Living Room, he expressed his feelings for other men and women in the shelter in terms of family:

> It's like describing my family, my brothers and my sisters. They're all good people. You know it's just like your family. We look out for each other, pretty much. If one person gots one thing and another person needs it, we kind of shift. It is like one big happy family. Everybody gets along together. Yea, you have your undesirables in here, but on the up and up, everybody gets along with each other pretty much. I mean, everybody pretty much does what they can for everybody and on the general basis of a loving environment basically speaking. It is the same deal as "do unto others as they do unto you," that's the way we work it.

When asked to describe the social atmosphere of The Living Room, DJ also used family terms in his description. He commented, "it is like a family type situation. Just like you feel at home."

While many road dogs and loners expressed feelings of kinship among the homeless, using the label family was not sufficient grounds to apply the label of fictive kin. In the following section, it will be argued that although feelings of solidarity are more common in generalized exchange networks (Uehara 1990), long-term restricted exchanges found in this study more closely resembled familial relationships and therefore were more fitting of the term fictive kin. It is not being argued that research by Wagner (1993), Rivlin and Imbimbo (1989), Stack (1974), and others did not identify fictive kin relationships. Such studies have been groundbreaking and inspiring to this study. While Stack (1974), Dordick (1997) and others identified more long-term networks, the groups described in the present study were extremely fluid and fragile. For example, members of the group camping outside The Living Room practiced generalized exchanges and some mentioned a sense of solidarity with each other, but no real loyalty or trust seemed to develop between group members. In fact, loners and road dogs were just as likely to express a healthy dose of caution when describing other shelter guests. Respondents were quite clear that not everyone lived by the presumed code of the streets. Danny, who has had years of experience on the streets of many cities stated, "There are people that absolutely cannot be trusted on the street." When asked to describe his relationships with other homeless men, Marty, Chris's road dog, replied, "I mean, I've got friends that I would ask favors of, but I wouldn't turn my back on them."

Troy, who has been on and off the streets for twenty years, repeatedly stated he did not trust the other homeless who spent time in The Living Room. When asked what he thought when others described the shelter as a "family-like atmosphere." He quickly rebutted:

> I would say that's crap. I'd say most of the people that hang out here all day just tolerate each other. There are near fights every day here amongst these "family members." There are a few individuals who won't forgive and forget. They'll hold a grudge and pay it back later. That's why you see people out here with a black eye. If I had a family like this, I'd stop seeing my family.

Theme analysis of the interview transcripts revealed that generalized exchanges were practiced among groups and even between members of the larger population that frequented The Living Room. When describing these generalized exchange relationships, some informants expressed feelings of solidarity towards other homeless individuals, and the group as a whole, but such sentiments tended to overemphasize the strength of the generalized ties. As Dordick points out, when friendships are formed out of the need for help, the aid can become the sole basis for the friendship. A more descriptive classification of the general homeless community evolving out of The Living Room might not only include examples of general aid, but it might also be expressed as "Don't fuck with me and I won't fuck with you" (Snow and Anderson 1993). Danny's description of his interactions with other homeless men is quite telling of this sentiment, "I talk to them, joke around with them, but I don't like them at all." As a result, the street networks in this study that formed around this philosophy were generally weak networks of acquaintances that likely expressed a solidarity based on common experiences and were temporary in nature.

I Got Me a Road Dog

Once connections to families of origin, created families, and generalized exchange between the homeless had been tapped, loners had nowhere but agencies and their inner strength to turn. Homeless who were willing to partner up, on the other hand, had one more option. Partnering up with a road dog provided another avenue for support on the street. According to Chris, who first explained the concept of road dogs to me, it is a rather guarded term. He explained that terms like tramp were commonly used around those who had homes, but road dogs and other such terms were generally reserved for conversations between the homeless. Road dogs partnered up with the goal of making life on the street easier. Being, or having, a road dog can mean different things to different men. There were road dogs in the study that had only partnered up a few times during years on the street and some men who had more road dogs than they could remember. Generally, road dogs took two forms, "road dogs for the journey" and "lifelong road dogs." Road dogs for the journey were in essence traveling partners. They were exchange-based relationships that were short-lived and did not reach the level of fictive kin. Lifelong road dogs were a different variety. Lifelong road dog relationships were also restricted exchange relationships but typically lasted for a greater period of time. They were called lifelong road dogs not because they last for a lifetime, but because the partners believed that if they ever separated, which happened in the vast majority of cases, they would be able to team up again without skipping a beat. Lifelong road dogs also developed a level of intimacy far beyond what road dogs for the journey were able to achieve. Despite their classification, both categories of road dogs begin as exchange-based partnerships with survival as their goal.

Partnering up made life easier because road dogs were able to exchange resources with each other. While road dogs, like most homeless, practiced generalized exchanges under the code of the streets, the exchanges between partners were restricted in nature. Restricted exchanges, as explained by Ekeh (1974), take place between two partners and were based on a quid pro quo mentality. Because the exchanges are typically governed by direct reciprocity, Ekeh (1974) contends such arrangements do not typically generate feelings of solidarity between partners. That assumption has been challenged. According to Lawler and Yoon (1993), as well as Kollock (1994), dyadic exchanges between strangers were found to produce feelings of commitment, trust, attachment, and obligation. Scanzoni and Marsiglio (1993) argue that restricted exchanges have the potential for producing instability, but as was the case with lifelong road dogs, partners could be regarded as family after practicing restricted exchanges over an extended period.

Why Partners Were Sought

When a homeless man in this study found someone he could trust, with whom he shared a common goal, he often partnered up for survival reasons. Before these men reached that point, there were typically two things missing from their lives that encouraged them to partner up. Because most road dogs had nowhere else to turn, and few resources of their own, they sought partners to help acquire resources to better suit them for survival on the street.

Lack of Family Ties. As evident from the informants, support from family members was scarce to nonexistent. Although road dogs had slightly higher levels of contact and support than loners, road dogs still did not do well in that area. Only nineteen of the thirty-three road dogs had been in contact in the last year with any parents or siblings and most contact was described as quite infrequent at best. In terms of created kin, twenty road dogs were fathers but only nine had contact with their children in the past year. With the exception of a few cases, ex-wives and ex-girlfriends were not even contacted, let alone a source of developing exchange relationships. When asked if he could rely on his family for help, Mark, who had nothing to do with them, replied:

> Forget them. Blood will burn you quicker than your friends will. Other brothers and sisters will try to burn you. Money-wise or whatever, they try to take it from you. My ex-wife she's no good. They all want everything. My wife is money hungry. Money hungry. Taught my kids how to be money hungry. I want nothing to do with that ok. These guys here, road dogs, like I said you've got to find the right one. There are only one or two that are pretty good. As far as my road dogs go, we're family. I would consider that dude as one of my brothers, one of my own real brothers. He never tried to burn me. I'd prefer him any day to family and other friends. Any day. Any day.

Trevor, a home guard who partnered with Barry, was able to see his created family more than most informants, but he was still unable to rely on them for the type of support he often needed. When asked who he felt closest to in his life, Trevor replied:

> Road dogs like Barry. That is the one I got to depend on. Like I said when it is twenty below zero out here and I'm cold, I may not be able to get a hold of anybody in my family. I may not be able to get a hold of my friends. I know where he's at. I can tell you where he is at right now. That's my partner right there. I mean I can call my family. I can call my son right now and say are you going to be around tonight. He'll say, "Yea, where do you want me to be." But there's no guarantee that he'll be there because he's got other family arrangements. He's got two sisters, he's got a nephew, he's got a mother, and he's got a girlfriend. All of them can impose on his time. The same with friends. I got several really close friends that I haven't seen for two or three years. I mean these are twenty year friendships. I can call them up and ask them what they're doing, but if they've already made prior arrangements, I'm done. And I can't

blame them, but I can count on Barry. There's damn few people in the world
that I can count on and Barry is one of them.

Barry was also asked who the most important person in his life was and to
whom he felt the closest. Not surprisingly, his answer included his partner and
his children. Barry deliberated, "Well, it is kind of hard to say. I mean, probably
the most important one would be my running mate, Trevor, because I'm on the
street. My kids are the most important in my life but I don't see them that much
and being on the street you've got to depend on somebody that you're with."
Because road dogs like Trevor, Barry and Mark were unable or unwilling to
count on their traditional kin for support, they chose to partner up to make the
acquisition of resources easier.

Lack of Resources. If there was one lesson learned from talking with informants,
it was that the street was nowhere you would like to be. It is dirty, too cold or
too hot, too wet, and simply obtaining the things you needed to survive was a
constant struggle. According to Randal, who became director of The Living
Room after Virginia stepped down, it was by necessity that most homeless became very good at surviving:

> Their dream is just getting by and surviving. That is who these people are, they
> are survivors. I always say that if the big bomb falls, these are the folks that are
> going to make it. It is not going to be the bankers and all of us it will be these
> folks because they have already done it. They have already survived on the
> streets. They know how to survive on the streets and they know how to take
> care of each other.

Survival on the streets, typically defined as the acquisition of resources, was the
main reason expressed for partnering up with another road dog. As described by
Keefe and Roberts, "Clearly, for those on the verge of destitution, reciprocity is
no abstract concept; it is indeed another word for survival" (1984, 121). Road
dogs in this study were found to exchange food, money, clothing, shelter, protection, information, and emotional support.

Overall, both loners and road dogs lacked intrinsic and extrinsic resources.
Not only was finding and keeping a blanket or a coat sometimes difficult, finding someone with whom you could rely on for emotional support was also a
challenge. Road dogs were often found to help fill the void. Road dog relationships were characterized by restricted exchanges because each partner relied
almost solely on the other for the acquisition of resources. That did not mean
that partners like Trevor and Barry only traded back and forth and what could be
achieved in that way was all that was acquired. Instead, Trevor and Barry sought
resources from a variety of individuals and locations and then shared their goods
with each other. A more pure example of their restricted partnership could be
found in their exchange of protection. No goods changed hands but each partner
knew they could rely on each other, and only each other, to watch their back

while sleeping out each night. They worked as a team to survive, because as Trevor stated, "Everybody needs somebody else one time or another. They can't make it on their own."

Road dogs, as just described, do not fit the exact model of restricted exchange relationships described by Ekeh (1974). More realistically, Uehara (1990) suggested that exchanges should be thought of on a continuum from restricted to generalized exchange. Following Uehara (1990), road dog relationships more closely resembled restricted exchange partnerships. Social exchange theory also maintains that exchange relationships must be of value to each party and possess a balance of reciprocity.

Since relationships must be of value to each party, it is also assumed that each individual is joining a relationship to maximize their benefits. Therefore, homeless men partnered up in order to exchange things that they lacked. Paul learned about the value of friends in maximizing personal benefit long before he was homeless. Paul repeated a lesson from his father:

> People always look at me and say, "God, you're so quiet and you're always so alone." I don't get into crowds and I don't let people pick me for a friend. I pick them. I am not being a snob or nothing. It is just that I know what I want in a friend, someone to relate to and to spend time with. My dad taught me a long time ago that you should see finding a friend as a very valuable thing. He told me if you get a friend it should be for two reasons. One, because you get along and enjoy the person. The other reason is he has got something you want. Whether he's got a little more knowledge in something you want to learn about or whatever. But that friendship has to be of value to you and to him. You can pick his brain and that makes you a better person. That's why I don't hang around with a lot of these guys that just sit around and do nothing. They have no desire to go anywhere, do anything, or do better.

The importance of a balance of reciprocity and value to each partner was also demonstrated by Marty. According to Marty, road dogs partnered up initially because they wanted something. He explained how these relationships were different than friends:

> They're (road dogs) based on need instead of want. Everybody wants friends. It's nice to have somebody to talk to, but when your stomach is hungry or you're out of cigarettes or your water bottle is empty, there has to be somebody to go to. It's kind of like we're one person because we do, you know the same things, but yet there is a need for each other. You know, I play my role, he plays his role, and it kind of works out to where we get the job done. It's kind of unspoken with Chris and I. We know what we have to do.

The importance of reciprocity and maximum benefit were also discussed in terms of what types of individuals would not make good partners. Ben, who had not seen his family for over twenty years, pointed out that most men avoided taking a road dog that did not live by the code of the streets. By paying attention to those around him, he knew which men he would not form relationships with.

"You remember who is always bumming cigarettes and then you see maybe a pack in their pocket and they're just smoking everybody else's and not their own. And then there are people that will bum cigarettes. . . . cigarettes are a big thing around here. . . . and then you see them with a $50 bag of dope or a pull a fifty out of their pocket, you never forget that." Failure to reciprocate could cause more problems than impacting potential traveling partners. Dordick (1997) also cited a general distrust between group members at the Station in regards to reciprocity when it came to money. Willmott (1987) called the failure to reciprocate a betrayal of trust, which on the street it could be deadly. Ricky explained the care with which the homeless men guard their belongings. "Our gear is all we have you know. Even though we want to share our things with another person, you don't just start taking stuff from us. You could get killed for stealing just a cigarette or something. You could get killed for that stuff."

After reviewing social support literature, Gottleib (1983) argued, "Exposure to adversity prompts a need for contact and social comparison with similar peers who augment or redirect the individual's coping efforts by marshaling cognitive, affective, and material resources" (1983, 207). Exactly what resources were exchanged through redirected coping efforts will be discussed in the section on road dogs for the journey. This topic, however, cannot be addressed before addressing the question of how road dog relationships formed.

How Partnerships Form

Proximity. According to the general literature on friendship formation and mate selection, proximity plays a large role in relationship formation. In short, individuals are most likely to develop relationships with those with whom they come in the most contact (Saegert et al. 1973; Homans 1961; Festinger, Schachter and Back 1963). In the homeless community this translates into many contact factors such as the preferred soup kitchen, preferred shelter or camp site, and whether an individual tended to be transient or not. In studying homeless youth, McCarthy et al. (2002) found that relationships were often formed among youth who frequently congregated at the same street corners, shopping malls, or parks. Once the homeless find themselves in a common location such as The Living Room, social exchange theorists hypothesize a system of carefully considering potential friends or partners.

Two Beginnings. As explained by social exchange theory, the acquisition of friends and partners is a calculated process based on potential benefits that may be provided by the other actor. Secord and Backman (1964) explain that when a group of strangers meet, each person samples interaction with a number of different actors in search of the actor who would provide the highest profit level. According to Secord and Backman (1964), when both partners are able to maximize rewards and minimize costs, exchange partnerships often result and lead to feelings of commitment.

Using social exchange theory as the model, road dog relationships typically formed in one of two ways. According to Scanzoni and Marsiglio (1993), social ties develop on a group level based on generalized exchanges. They argue intrinsic exchanges of sociability lead to extrinsic exchanges of goods. On the group level, Scanzoni and Marsiglio (1993) contend that such arrangements can produce arrangements of fictive kin. A small number of road dog partnerships stemmed from larger group activity. Trevor and Barry were one of the few road dogs in the study that began this way. Trevor detailed how they came to partner up: "I've known Barry for ten years. The first five years I knew him we were just drinking buddies running into each other here and there. We would say 'Hi' and shit like that. Over the last four or so years we've just developed this bond." Trevor and Barry's relationship developed from acquaintances, to a restricted exchange partnership, and finally to a relationship that I will later argue should be considered fictive kin.

The second, and more common way road dog relationships formed was simply meeting someone compatible and forming a relationship based on the exchange of intrinsic resources such as food, clothing, shelter, and protection. Chris, Marty's road dog, explained this process in practical terms:

> Ok, what you do once you come into a town you try to find somebody you are compatible with and that you can carry a conversation with. You find somebody that likes the same things. Then you're not alone any more. Then the next thing you build up from acquaintances to friends. It's hard to trust a person for a while until you get to know them, especially sleeping outside with them. But once you finally do that (trust them) you start to share everything. Then bam, there you are, you are working as a team.

The majority of road dog relationships became restricted partnerships but lasted for only a limited time. As Chris went on to explain, the partners were working towards a goal, but "unfortunately most of the time the goal is enough money for a bus ticket to somewhere else. Then you never see them again." Such partnerships were labeled road dogs for the journey. Occasionally, road dogs that started in the way Chris described moved forward and become relationships in which both extrinsic and intrinsic resources were exchanged in a restricted partnership. In fact, Chris and Marty fit this category. Over time, these relationships develop into arrangements of fictive kin, called lifelong road dogs.

Similar Characteristics and Values. When homeless men sought road dogs they were compatible with, the resulting partnerships were typically between men of similar ages, values, and the same race. Road dogs were asked if age mattered when they selected a partner. Almost every informant replied similarly to Kent who stated, "Age doesn't really matter. We're both human beings and we are both trying to survive on the streets." Despite comments like Kent's, the vast majority of partnerships described by road dogs were between men of similar age.

This was the case with the selection of running mates among road dogs. The criteria for common values and characteristics were typically expressed not in terms of the types of men they sought out, but rather the types of men with whom they would not partner up. Mark relayed his three groups of men he would not partner up with and how he distinguished them from viable partners:

> One, punks. . . . gays in other words. Two, thieves, druggies, and people that don't work. Three, people that try to get over on other people. You can tell real quick by talking to them. The best way to do it is to get them drunk. If they drink 1, 2, or 3 beers and start to think they are big and bad and talking garbage, they are no good. If you can get a man like me who can drink and drink and drink and act like it's still his first beer, that's a cool dude. That's how I determine who's who. You see, my father always said you pick your friends, don't let them pick you. It's true.

The avoidance of homosexuals was expressed in many interviews. As Cleve felt compelled to clarify when describing his relationship with a road dog, "You get more intimate, more on a personal basis. Not intimate like in a love relationship, but intimate as a stronger friendship." Perhaps because most road dogs relayed that they slept in close proximity to each other, they felt the need to demonstrate that they were heterosexual. Asserting the fact that they were not only heterosexual, but bragging about their sexual prowess was also expressed when informants were asked about the sharing of resources. It was not uncommon for road dogs to reply that they shared everything but their women.

Race also played an important role in the consideration of potential partners. While only one respondent, Cameron, said that he would not partner up with "blacks and Mexicans," the vast majority of partnerships included men of the same race. Of the thirty-three road dogs in the sample, and their multiple partners, only two cross-racial partnerships were mentioned. Mark had partnered up with one white man for a short time. While Mark did not express that the race of his running mate was an issue, Matt presented a situation in which race seemed to matter. Matt, who was white, partnered with a black man he called Dog while he was in California. According to Matt, this led to some troubles:

> He's a black guy, an African American guy and white people don't like that. They think if a white man goes to look for a partner, he should pick a white person and a black person should pick a black person. We got threatened. There was a bunch of people that wanted to take us on. But because of Dog, who he was and how many friends he had, they didn't go up against us. When Dog got picked up for drugs and sent to jail I was told by some of his friends that it was time to leave town. I was told that I could come back when Dog gets out.

Trevor and Barry were probably the most stellar examples of similar characteristics. Trevor described his running mate Barry while also demonstrating why he felt protection was an important aspect of partnering up:

Yea, I have a partner. His name is Barry. He is fifty-four, about my age. He's been on the streets for about as long as I have. He's got the same situation (both home guards. . . . divorced. . . . kids. . . . alcoholics). We're not bums like most of these guys. Most of them partner up to make money. We partner up because if we don't, you can get your head kicked in. Take a look at what happened here last night (a man sleeping outside The Living Room was severely beaten by another homeless man). Ouch, man. One of the biggest problems with the homeless is homeless people stealing from homeless people. So we partner up that way nobody can gang up on us. You know, partners come and go with a lot of these guys. The true transients, they get up, boogie, and you don't see them for a year. They just want to travel around the country. This is my home. This is where I live. This is where we live. We have both lived here all our lives basically. Thirty-some years!

As a theme analysis of the interview data revealed, relationships were able to form because potential running mates found themselves in the same location and were able to offer some type of benefit to each other. Street partnerships stemmed from both social connections and a simple desire to exchange. In addition to profitable exchange, partnerships were also formed around similar values and characteristics. The process of evaluating potential partners ranged from an afternoon to years. Ricky explained how he usually approached the process:

You know you've got to be able to sit there and mentally evaluate and assess the situation. You've got to assess the person's mentality first of all. Is he going to be a drunk? Is he schizophrenic? Does he just nut-up at the drop of a hat? You don't just hop on a train or hop on the highway with somebody you've never met in your life. You have to be around them for a day or two at least to be able to see what type of person they are. It's not something that you can just do overnight. Let me ask you this, if you were in the middle of New York City would you walk up to somebody in Central Park at midnight and say, "I need you to go down to the store and buy me a bottle of booze. All I've got is a hundred dollar bill." Of course not! There's your answer. You've got to be able to know the person. You've got to know exactly what you're dealing with before you even think of getting out there and going with a stranger somewhere. I usually know what this guy is going to be like in three or four days. I will know if this guy is compatible or if he's got a couple screws loose.

Road Dogs for the Journey: Lessons in Dissolution

It has been explained why and how road dogs formed, but the reality is that although extremely helpful, most partnerships did not last very long. Most road dogs did not reach the status of lifelong or fictive kin but instead parted company at the end of the journey.

As demonstrated in the previous section, road dog relationships were generally based on restricted exchange. According to Ekeh (1974), tension and instability frequently characterize restricted exchange relationships and they last only for a short duration. This was the case with most partnerships described by the road dogs in the study. Road dog relationships typically dissolved after a short time for five general reasons. While the first reason only applied to road dogs for the journey, the remaining reasons also applied to lifelong road dogs. Road dogs for the journey typically ceased running together because they were formed with the intention of only securing a temporary traveling companion. Eric demonstrated how the term road dog was used on the street. According to Eric, you say, "I got me a road dog. I got me somebody to travel with. A partner to travel with." Coulter, who had been traveling for years, explained that road dogs for the journey typically formed for protection or around a common goal such as drinking. He described most of his road dogs as good people he could share a drink with. "Usually drunks. Usually the people I travel with are pretty good people. I've never had nobody rob me or anything like that. It's usually for a couple days or a week or two. Then he goes his way and I go mine. I get a road dog for safety measures or whatever it could be. Most times you end up drinking a lot. That's mostly what it is."

Because they did not run together long enough to establish a relationship based on anything but the exchange of resources, most road dogs did not develop a bond or attachment that would allow leniency regarding unbalanced exchanges. Ben described what happened when a road dog did not hold up their end of the bargain, "Most of the time you don't keep a tab of who is contributing more. If it gets out of hand and you find that it's a one-sided deal where you are always fronting the thing, you kind of give the guy a little bit of incentive. But you don't chew him out. Nine times out of ten it works. If not, you move on."

Differing goals were also commonly offered as an explanation for relationship dissolution. According to Marty, road dogs partnered up with different goals in mind. One may want to get to California while the other was planning on stopping in Plainview to work for a while. In these cases, road dogs usually continued partnering until they get to a fork in the road. Sometimes road dogs adjusted their plans. For example, the partner who was trying to get to California may decide to stop in Plainview and work for a while in the hope that their partner would continue on with them at a later date. Ultimately their goals became no longer compatible and different paths are taken.

Because road dogs were not only based on an exchange of resources, but also on a need for companionship, it was not surprising that when one partner started a relationship with a woman, the road dog relationship ended in most cases. Terrance, who had been traveling for years when he was interviewed, explained what happened to the road dog he had last winter, "The only reason I'm not running with him now is he got a girlfriend. I just stay out of their life. He has his things to do so I don't step in there." This did not happen in all the cases. TC was the only informant that was married and had contact with his spouse. TC lived on the streets with his wife but he maintained his relationship with Taz, his lifelong road dog. On occasion he left his wife and traveled with him. When discussing the relationship, TC said: "There is nothing in the world that is going to change that that's my brother, that's my partner, that's my friend for life. My wife is not going to come between that. She knows that. She is in total agreement with that." According to TC, he does not have to be with Taz every day but they will be partners until the day one or both of them die. "That's just an acceptable fact."

The fifth reason partnerships ended was because of an argument. Arguments covered the range of the previous four examples. Arguments over goals, plans, values, women, and money were quite common. Jacob described why his four year partnership broke off the summer before:

> I had a friend that I was hitchhiking with. I'd had no problems buddying up with him but I guess some people change. Either I changed, or he changed, or we both changed. Anyway, he turned around and started putting people against me when we came here (Plainview). When we were on the road everything was cool, but when we came here he turned kind of sadistic. I think he got trapped in it because now he is in prison.

If these relationships survived the many obstacles placed in front of them, they often moved into another stage. After running together for at least a few months, road dogs began to develop relationships that were no longer based solely on exchange. These relationships were termed lifelong road dogs.

Lifelong Road Dogs: Fictive Kin of the Street

Most homeless men in the study took a running mate at least once, but the majority of those relationships ended rather quickly. On a rare occasion, road dogs formed on the basis of exchange and grew into partnerships that were no longer based simply on exchange and could last for years. Most road dogs in the study had one or three partners that could be considered lifelong partners during their months or years on the street.

Lifelong road dogs were not partners for life but rather partners that had been together for an extended period of time and believed if they ever separated they would be able to team up again without skipping a beat. Being able to resume the relationship immediately was generally explained in family terms by offering explanations such as Ricky's, "If we ever meet again it would be like we never missed a beat, like brothers." Chris, who now has a lifelong road dog in Marty, described his feelings about his past road dogs:

> I would never compare them (typical friends) with these friends (road dogs). Road dogs are more like family. In my whole lifetime, on and off the road, I've got seven road dogs. There's seven people out of all these people that I have met, that I, even today, if I seen them and I won the lotto and had an RV or anything, I'd stop and pick them up and welcome them into any part of my life. And all the rest of them, the hundreds and hundreds of people you meet, I wouldn't do that.

While most road dogs professed the ability to immediately link up with a lifelong road dog they had lost contact with, Chuck, a rail tramp, actually had that opportunity. About seven years earlier, Chuck traveled with a lifelong road dog for a year before they parted company. A few years after Chuck's road dog came through Plainview. According to Chuck, they partnered up a few days later and traveled for the next several months. Eventually Chuck returned to Plainview and his lifelong road dog, a full-time tramp, returned to the road. If their paths ever cross again, Chuck stated they would certainly hit the road again.

Among the informants who were partnered up with a lifelong road dog, the feeling was that even if they got off the streets they would take their partner with them. Barry, in speculating about what he would do if he got off the street, concluded that he would take his road dog. "Once I got on my feet or got an apartment, I would ask him to move in until he could find something. No, I would never break it off because we have gone through too much together."

Acting Like Kin: A Case for New Action Theory

Whether they had been together for years like Barry and Trevor, or ran together for a year and parted, lifelong road dogs developed a level of intimacy far beyond what road dogs for the journey were able to achieve. Lifelong road dogs were also found to be more encompassing in their responsibilities, more interdependent, and have a higher tolerance for periods on unbalanced exchange. Under these circumstances, social exchange theory was no longer sufficient in explaining partnerships between homeless men. Social exchange theory explained why homeless men partnered up, but new action theory provided a more encompassing way to view these relationships. New action theory, therefore, was employed to demonstrate how fictive kinships formed as an adaptation to the harsh reality of the street and an absence of traditional family support. This lens allowed for the possibility that lifelong road dogs could be considered family, or fictive kin, based on the perspective of each partner and the actions performed by the dyad.

Blood (1972) points out that individuals living in harsh economic circumstances are more likely to have fictive kin relationships because they are forced to draw on the aid of others. Because the homeless have little material and social capital, they frequently turn to others in the same situation. Occasionally, these relationships reach a level in which they can be described as fictive kin. Fictive kin are persons who are treated like relatives but who are not related by blood or marriage (Chatters et al. 1994). Using this simple definition, an argument can be made that lifelong road dogs took on many responsibilities and provided each other with levels of intimacy and support typically relegated to families of origin and creation. In essence, lifelong road dogs acted like kin. Actions indicative of kin status included performing the functions and exchanges usually maintained by kin, the willingness to accept unbalanced partners, and the use of family language to describe partners.

New action theory recognizes that living arrangements are constructed in response to changing social environments. These living arrangements may develop into primary groups. According to Scanzoni and Marsiglio (1993), a sense of being part of a family, or fictive family, can develop out of extrinsic and intrinsic interdependencies regardless of blood or legal ties. Because new action theory views the family as a socially constructed entity (Rice 1994), it is a useful perspective from which to view partnerships between lifelong road dogs.

Road dogs were found to exchange and provide intrinsic and extrinsic resources including food, clothing, shelter, money, information, and emotional support. What was apparent was that these exchanges did not have to be tit for tat in accordance with a strict accounting of restricted exchanges. For example, situations were common in which one partner would search out food while the other would be working day labor to buy gas money, alcohol, or other items. Most road dogs looked at it as a team approach like Marty described earlier. In essence, Marty and Chris had separate roles and knew what each needed to accomplish to meet their shared goals. Lifelong road dog relationships also allowed for unbalanced exchanges, providing, in essence, an insurance policy to both partners. Dave, a twenty-seven-year-old road dog who had been homeless since his mother died eight years earlier, explained how he viewed resources such as food, cigarettes, and beer: "He do what he got to do to get food and I do what I have to do and we just put it in one bag. That's how it is on the road because you've got to look out for each other. Because one might not be able to do so good one day, but that doesn't mean he didn't do nothing." Dave's description of how direct exchange was not always necessary is an example of how lifelong road dog relationships shift over time to partnerships not based solely on exchange.

Extrinsic Interdependencies. Extrinsic resources, according to Scanzoni and Marsiglio (1993), included money, goods, and services. Extrinsic resources commonly exchanged by road dogs included information, food, clothing, shelter, and money.

Information was one of the most valued commodities on the street. This was especially true when one of the road dogs was new to the area or had only recently become homeless. Troy had been homeless twenty years earlier, but when he returned to the street a few months before the interview, it was a different place. Troy revealed the help his road dog gave him during his adjustment and what he exchanged for the information:

> I didn't have a lot of experiences when I did it twenty years ago. We applied for various programs together and he taught me the ropes again on how to survive. Now I could lose my life doing the wrong thing at the wrong time. And he (road dog) has kind of taught me the ropes of surviving which has been a great benefit to me. Of course I haven't learned all the lessons that I would like to. I lost all my gear two weeks ago. Obviously if I had been listening a little closer I probably wouldn't have lost that gear. It's things like that he's explained to

me as we go along. I don't know what he gets from me other than I am a generous guy. If he's out of cigarettes, I will bum him one. I'll buy him a pop. I bought him breakfast the other day and I'll do things for him.

Food and clothing, very necessary items, were not exchanged as much as expected. They were traded and provided less frequently because they could be acquired through The Living Room and other agencies. When a meal was missed, lifelong road dogs certainly looked out for each other and whoever had money at the time bought something to share. Clothing was also free or within the means of most homeless that frequented The Living Room because the thrift store located in the same building would allow anyone to work off their purchases. The exchange of clothing, and even food, usually happened when items were found or scavenged. In these cases, if what was acquired did not fit the person finding it, or they did not need it, their road dog received "first dibs." Jerry and his road dog were the exception and actually shared most of their clothing. Jerry mentioned:

> We wear exactly the same size too so when we would go tramping we'd go to who ever had clean clothes and put some in a bag and take them with us. As a matter of fact, he gave me this coat because it was getting warm last spring and he said, "Here, take this coat." He told me he would rather trust me with it than somebody else. He got another coat this winter so he told me to keep this coat because he knew I liked it for duck hunting because it is camouflage.

Because there were few options for housing in Plainview for single males who did not want, or need, to enter a substance abuse or religious program, shelter was a coveted resource. Shelter was repeatedly exchanged by revealing secret openings to a building or letting your road dog sleep in your car. Shelter was also provided when one road dog found a friend with whom to crash. In these cases, it was sometimes asked if their partner could also crash there for the night. For example, Randy met a woman in Colorado while he was traveling with his lifelong road dog. When the woman asked Randy if he would like to stay at her house for the night, he replied: "I got a partner and I can't leave him on the streets you know." After some convincing, she put the two men up for a couple of nights. Given the finding that establishing relationships with women was often cited as a reason for terminating street partnerships, this event demonstrated the importance of Randy's road dog to him.

Money was treated differently than other resources. When one road dog had more money they were expected to purchase necessary items, but money was not shared like food and cigarettes. If money was loaned between road dogs, unlike other items, repayment was expected. Barry explained how money was handled with Trevor: "With me and Trevor, it's not like if I go and make $50 I go and give him $25. If I've got some money and he needs a pack of cigarettes, I will buy them for him, but we don't give each other like $10 or $20 unless it is an emergency or something like that." There were few exceptions to this rule, one being when your road dog ended up in jail. Two informants mentioned paying visits and sending money to their road dogs who had been arrested. Mark had traveled with a road dog for a year and a half when their "shoplift-and-return" venture turned sour. Mark's road dog was caught and sentenced to ten years in prison because he had several additional warrants. Later, Mark went to prison to visit his partner and left him $300, which was half of Mark's money.

After detailing the list of extrinsic exchanges, one thing stands out. The resources that were exchanged were extremely helpful, but there was not much variety in what could be offered. When Barry was asked if there was anything that he could not ask Trevor for, he pondered, "I don't know. I guess I really never thought of it. The only way we deal is cigarettes or booze or five dollars. Nothing very big. We don't have anything big right now." Two aspects of Barry's comments were very interesting. First, throughout the interview Barry talked about a host of less tangible resources like support and protection but he did not mention them when summing up what was exchanged. It should also be noted that Barry used the term "we" when explaining that they didn't have anything big at the moment. Barry and Trevor were one of the most intimate and long-running partners in the study. They have known each other for ten years and have been running together for the last four years.

Intrinsic Interdependencies. Because only a small range of tangible resources were exchanged, intrinsic support became even more important. Intrinsic resources found in the study included protection, emotional support, and a social outlet. Protection was one of the most commonly cited resources exchanged between partners and the use of family terms made it clear to others that road dogs would stick up for each other. This was a seen as a sound strategy given that crime against those on the street and between the homeless was on the minds of many informants. Even though the code of the streets was cited by many informants, not all were governed by its principles. Lee and Schreck (2005) connect the prevalence of homeless on homeless crime as a product of physical propinquity, minimal guardianship, and the perceived low chance of facing sanctions.

Protection could be categorized as a service, and thus an extrinsic resource, but most road dogs expressed protection more in terms of a secure feeling that allowed them to sleep at night. Stan described a situation outside The Living Room that took place about a month before the interview, in which his road dog may have saved his life. He explained that there was a tramp, "some kind of psycho," who was convinced he was a government hit man sent to eliminate him. "It was starting to get a little scary but Ronnie was behind me. He made it clear he was my partner." According to Stan, Ronnie was worried that the homeless "psycho" was going to knife Stan when the two were apart so they always stuck together until the "psycho" left town. After detailing what Ronnie had done for him, Stan looked directly in my eyes and said: "You don't run into too many people that are going to take a knife for you. I mean, do you have anybody that would take a knife for you?"

Stan and Ronnie's relationship did not focus on simply watching each other's back. He also relayed how Ronnie provided a social outlet as well. When asked why he partnered up with Ronnie, Stan said he was easy to talk to and made him laugh from the very beginning. "He was a fun guy. You didn't feel homeless around him because you were always doing something or going someplace. You know, just having coffee down here was an event. I really miss Ronnie." They traveled together for the summer but the fact that Stan was a home guard and Ronnie loved to tramp led to an eventual parting of company. Like most lifelong road dogs, they had general plans for Ronnie to swing back through Plainview the following summer and pick up Stan for another "run of the circuit."

Intrinsic resources also included emotional support. This was one of the resources that appeared to be very important to the men, but also something most did not feel comfortable talking about. When the subject of emotional support was breached, many road dogs like Chuck, who has been living under a bridge for years, simply replied, "Just someone to talk to. Someone to tell what is happening in our lives and what's going on."

What was provided and exchanged between lifelong road dogs was limited but extremely important. It was also relevant that resources usually acquired through the family such as food, clothing, shelter, protection, and so on had to be secured through another homeless man. The lack of exchanges between informants and more traditional sources of family support is why the label fictive kin is appropriate for lifelong road dogs. It was not simply that the partner helped purchase food, but that their partner was often the only person in their life who was even remotely acting like a family member.

Accepting Unbalanced Relationships

The description of resource acquisition to this point has been couched in the language of social exchange theory. While virtually all road dog relationships began as restricted exchange partnerships, over time some began to resemble partners who looked out for each other, rather than looking out for what could be exchanged. After being together for a considerable amount of time, lifelong road dogs began to accept when a partner no longer contributed equally to the arrangement. Such a shift demonstrated the fact that emotional support became as important, if not more important, than economic support. Therefore, the second justification for terming lifelong road dogs as fictive kin relationships can be found in the shift from exchange partnerships to sharing partners. According to Trevor, "There's none of this, it's your turn or it's my turn. It's whatever we got we share. It's the only way you can have a relationship. In a way it's like a husband and a wife. We share everything. If he needs something and I got it, it's his."

While all lifelong road dogs claimed to tolerate a certain level of imbalance in their arrangements, two informants revealed partnerships where one road dog basically took care of the other. Jerry explained his relationship with his lifelong road dog, Tom:

> I seen him about seven or eight years ago. Some guys come over to my place (when he was housed temporarily) and they had him with them. He was so tired that he just sat down on the couch and went to sleep for four or five hours. Over the years I got to know him. He has a lot of physical and other problems and stuff. I always felt bad. They (government) wouldn't give him social security. He maybe has a learning disability or something like that but he's a good guy. When I had a place he would come over and eat. He really appreciated it because he can't read good enough to follow directions. He was over at my place one time and he said, "Jerry, cook me something to eat why don't you." I told him to cook something so he got out some pancake mix. All you had to do was add water but he just looked at the picture on the box and tried to make them. They were scrambled and they had cream in the middle of them but I went ahead and ate them anyway. I didn't want to hurt his feelings. Since then I have done most of the cooking.

Later in the interview Jerry discussed how he would also drive Tom to where he needed to go and how he generally found the places where they could sleep. When asked what he got out of the relationship, Jerry replied:

> I get to relive all the days that was fun. I get to do some fun things. Because there's a lot of heartache on the street but there's a lot of happy times too. So I try to make some of them happy times happen. Like if Tom was going to walk on the streets, I would take him in my pickup because it doesn't use much gas. Then we go to McDonald's and drink coffee for a couple hours and things like that.

In addition to Marty and Chris, another lifelong road dog pair, Dave and Carter, both participated in the study. Carter, who was much older than Dave, took care of him and helped him learn how to survive. According to Dave, Carter has taught him how to hop a train, how to travel as light as possible, how to survive the elements, and other tricks of the trade. Carter went into greater detail about how he helped Dave. While traveling, Dave got into a fight and was sent to jail for three months. Because they had been traveling together for over a year, he did not abandon him. Instead, Carter went to work with a road crew and sent some of his money to Dave so he could buy cigarettes and toiletries. During both interviews, it became obvious that Dave was quite dependent on Carter. Carter explained that he would get annoyed sometimes because Dave was constantly on his elbow. After Carter expressed that he sometimes got frustrated with Dave and all he had to do for him, he was asked what he received from the relationship. As was the case with Jerry, Carter explained that he received emotional satisfaction for helping his friend:

It's gratification. It's helping somebody that needs help. He's handicapped in his brain. He can't hardly feed his ass. I get respect out of it. Since I left everyday society I haven't lost respect for myself, but I haven't done anything to rejuvenate it. I respect myself for doing this. So he gives me that. I get that kind of stuff in return. I get allegiance. Allegiance. You know, its good to have somebody that you allied with. Somebody that won't say for no reason, "I'm leaving now."

Most road dogs did not express unbalanced relationships with their lifelong partners to the extent of Jerry and Carter, but supporting a partner was not uncommon. Informants would routinely care for a sick partner, guard their positions, visit them in jail, and attempt to help them if they became depressed. When asked why they continued the relationships, the common responses were that they could not abandon a family member or that they had simply been through too much together.

Because lifelong road dogs provided each other with so many essential resources and because they did not expect direct reciprocity, they developed very strong bonds to each other. These bonds were repeatedly expressed in terms of family relationship.

Family Bonds and Terminology

Because this project focused on in-depth interviews with loners and road dogs as the main source of data, it is fitting that the final justification for classifying lifelong road dogs as fictive kin stemmed directly from the words of the informants. Although the terminology used to describe their feelings varied the message was consistent. Lifelong road dogs were considered family because they spent so much time together and because they were there for their partner. Walter, who sends money to his ex-wife and kids in El Paso, related that he considered a lifelong road dog family because of the amount of time they spend together and how close they became. "Just living day by day with each other. You know sharing everything that goes on like your problems. It's just like when you are sharing with your family. You're sharing with your closest buddy so they become family." Mark, whose road dog was in prison during the study, described why their relationship could survive the separation: "We are family that is it. We may fight with each other but when it comes down to really needing each other, we are there. That's what family is all about. I'd do the world for that man because my family would do it. I think he is the best partner I ever had."

It was particularly interesting that when road dogs referred to their partners as family, all but one pair used either the general label "family" or referred to their partner as a "brother." Other studies of fictive kin relationships found the use of terms like cousin or husband (Dordick 1997; Stack 1974), but road dogs in this study did not reveal the use of such terms. The one exception from this study was Carter and Dave's relationship. Carter, who is fifty years old, believed that Dave thought of him as a father figure. Carter's response when asked how close he was to Dave demonstrated his mixed emotions about their relationship: "I have no children. I think of him as a family member even though I resent the fact that he thinks of me as a father figure. But at the same time I have kind of mixed emotions. I do think of him as more or less a son figure. I resent the fact that he thinks of me as a father because I know I won't measure up." When Dave, twenty-seven years old, was asked in a separate interview to describe his relationship with Carter, he replied: "I want to say. . . . like. . . . he's older than me so he is like my uncle. He's like an uncle because he taught me things, you know. Like how to hop a train. I don't look at him as a father." Regardless of the specific use of terms, the reference to your partner as family sent a message to their road dog and the larger community that their relationship was significant.

The label fictive kin soundly applies to lifelong road dog relationships because they quite simply acted like family. The relatively long duration of the relationships, the functional roles they fulfilled, the intimacy of the relationships, the acceptance of unbalanced exchanges, and the fact that informants referred to their lifelong road dogs as family all lead to the conclusion that fictive kin is an appropriate description of lifelong road dogs.

Why They End

In theory, lifelong road dog relationships never end. In reality, they at least part company, and most do end. The dissolution of lifelong road dogs happens for the same reasons road dogs that partner up for the journey end. These relationships dissolve because of a heated argument, a patterned lack of reciprocity, one partner found a woman to hook up with, or simply because their goals led them in different directions.

The key distinction between the dissolution of lifelong and road dogs for the journey were found in the purpose of the partnership and in the degree of problem needed to separate the partners. Road dogs for the journey were often selected as a safety device for a short trip. When the trip ended, the vast majority of partnerships ended. If the journey was long or they decided to continue running together, the fact that the partnership was based on restricted exchange made them more susceptible to conflicts regarding unbalanced exchanges. Lifelong road dogs were also susceptible to the same arguments, changing goals, and "interfering women," but it took more to shake the foundation of the longer relationships. Because lifelong road dogs had progressed from exchange relationships to fictive kin, their ties were stronger and they would accept more turbulence in the relationship before abandoning it.

Given the important nature of lifelong road dog relationships, their reliance on each other, and the reference to each other as kin, how could they ultimately part company? This question was posed to road dogs in the interviews. Chris likened the parting of company between lifelong road dogs to a military transfer.

"Sometimes you just got to say, okay, that's it. It's like being in the military or something where the situation makes you break off the relationship. You get transferred and have to move. You've been together three years but there are times you've just got to get up and go."

Jerry, who watched out for his lifelong road dog, frequently left for a couple of weeks at a time to care for his ailing parents. He detailed how leaving family and friends was just something that occasionally had to be done:

> Well, it's like if you leave you just don't leave them in a bad way. Like if he Tom) was hurt or didn't have squat I couldn't leave him. I'd have to make sure he had clothes and a crashing place and stuff. But it's just like if you leave your family to do something. Sometimes you have to leave your friends too. And then The Living Room has a phone so I call back to get the news. We stay in touch. If he really needed something or was really hurt or something, I'd have to stick around to help him out, but as long as he's doing okay, I feel like I can go and do the things I need to do.

When put in those terms, the fact that lifelong road dogs parted company was not that foreign or surprising of a concept. Members of traditional families part company every day. Whether through divorce or simply a change of goals that moves one family member across the country, kin part company. However, that does not mean they were no longer kin or shared a bond. What distinguished members of traditional families from lifelong road dogs was the fact that once lifelong road dogs parted company, they only had the hope that someday their paths might cross again. Jerry's phone calls to Tom were generally unheard of among other lifelong road dog partnerships.

Conclusion

Both loners and road dogs practiced patterns of generalized exchange with other homeless individuals based on the concept of what comes around goes around. This concept presented itself as homeless looking out for each other by making sure their comrades were safe and warm. This concept was also applied between strangers. While many informants expressed a feeling of solidarity towards other homeless individuals, these relationships did not develop into strong ties such as those described by Dordick (1997), Uehara (1990), Jewell (1988), Gerstel and Gross (1987), Stack (1974), Liebow (1967), and Giallombardo (1966).

After tapping generalized exchanges as well as traditional family ties, loners had nowhere but agencies to turn for aid. Road dogs, however, frequently partnered up with another homeless man, creating restricted exchange relationships. These relationships took two forms. Road dogs for the journey were short-term partnerships based on an exchange of resources. They formed because informants generally lacked resources and traditional family connections to secure such resources. Such partnerships typically formed between individuals with similar characteristics and values.

Although lifelong road dogs formed in the same way, these partnerships lasted much longer and became more intimate. Because of the complex nature of lifelong road dogs, social exchange theory was not sufficient in detailing the relationships. New action theory was employed in order to view the construction of street partnerships as an adaptation to social and economic pressures. Under new action theory, the case was made that lifelong road dogs could be viewed as fictive kin relationships. The label fictive kin was appropriate for these relationships because in essence, they acted like families. That is, they provided intrinsic and extrinsic resources essential to survival, they protected their members, they lasted for a relatively significant period of time, they accepted unbalanced exchange partners, and most importantly, the informants viewed them as kin.

Chapter Eight

Beyond the Streets of Plainview

This study has given attention to three important issues which provide a better understanding of the lives and relationships of homeless men. Through analysis of interview and survey data from forty-five homeless men, levels of contact and exchange exhibited between homeless men and their families of origin and creation were assessed. In addition to the examination of traditional family ties, road dogs and loners were compared in relation to multiple facets of street life. The examination of road dogs and loners revealed men who faced daily challenges and hardships but were very resilient. The strength to face such constant adversity is a gift no person should have to use. The detailed focus of the study also revealed that while these men followed individual paths to homelessness, they shared many traits and experiences. Most importantly, the majority of informants lacked a strong family safety net that may have kept some of them off the streets.

Lessons from the Homeless Men of Plainview

Exchanging with Families of Origin and Creation

Study results indicate that the majority of the informants lacked consistent family contact and were even less likely to engage in exchange relationships. For example, 47 percent of respondents had no contact with any members of their family of origin in the year prior to the interview and only ten of the twenty-five fathers had any contact with their children in the past year. Not surprisingly, contacts with ex-wives and ex-girlfriends were almost non-existent. When contact was made with family members, it typically involved short phone calls to exchange information but rarely involved more than brief visits. When measuring levels of exchange, only meager exchanges were made between informants and their families of origin and even fewer were engaged in with their families of creation. For instance, only eleven respondents received any financial assistance from their families of origin and only two of the twenty-five fathers had made any attempt to financially support their children in the year prior to the interview. Besides exchanges of information, the most direct examples of exchange-based relationships were demonstrated when sons participated in household maintenance tasks in exchange for temporary shelter.

Given these findings, it might be tempting to label these men as disaffiliated, as Lafuente and Lane (1995), Baum and Burnes (1993), Rossi et al. (1986), and Spradley (1970) have labeled the homeless in their studies. However, as Blasi (1990) argues, the label implies that informants have stepped away from social contacts and may decide to affiliate again. Instead, Blasi (1990) maintains that the focus should be on the resources available to the homeless, including family ties and the impact of poverty. In agreement with Blasi, the focus of this research has been on examining the issues surrounding the meager levels of contact and exchange documented between homeless men and their families.

In addressing the limited levels of contact and exchange, two perspectives were utilized. The perspective of the informants, social exchange theory, and gender theory each contributed to a clearer picture as to why contact and exchanges were sparse. Drawing from social exchange theory allowed the focus to include the structural constraints placed on these men. Despite Rubin's (1985) contention that family members can usually be counted on for assistance even when no pattern of exchange has previously existed, the men in the study had little support to draw from. Social exchange theory also helped to establish a baseline for comparison of exchanges taking place between nonresident family members in the housed community. Hogan et al. (1993) estimated that half of Americans do not participate in exchange relationships with their parents. The baseline for comparison becomes even lower when gender is taken into account. Clear patterns have been found in the research that men are less involved than women in general kinkeeping (Furstenberg and Cherlin 1991), especially when it comes to non-custodial parenting (Silverstein and Bengston 1997).

The inclusion of both gender and social exchange theories highlighted the perspectives offered by informants as to the state of their family relationships. Informants noted that they had limited resources, lived long distances from their families, had burned several relationship bridges, experienced family disorganization, and had a general unwillingness to seek or provide support. Given these obstacles to the maintenance of family relationships, it was not surprising that contact and exchanges were limited. For example, one might not expect a great deal of opportunity for exchange to take place given that the mean physical distance between informants and family members was seven hundred miles. It was also not surprising that when exchanges did occur, transfers of information and emotional support were the most common forms of exchange. In summary, the informants' perspective, social exchange theory, and gender theory all contribute to greater understanding of why these men did not maintain strong family relationships.

Road Dogs and Loners

The classification and comparison of road dogs and loners, unique to this study, provided for descriptions of two different strategies for survival on the street. While road dogs and loners were similar in many ways, taking a road dog versus going it alone changed many aspects of street life. For instance, one of the major themes that surfaced in interviews with both road dogs and loners was the issue of trust. The concept, though, was approached from different angles. Road dogs set about partnering up by trying to weed out potential running mates, those they could trust, from homeless men they felt they could not turn their back on. Loners, on the other hand, were much more likely to assume that most homeless were not trustworthy and entered into social situations with that framework. This approach did not lead to total isolation among loners, but interview and survey data identified lower levels of affiliation among loners as compared to men willing to partner up.

When a homeless man willing to take on a partner found someone he could trust, the formation of a road dogs pair became a possibility. These partnerships were formed because the men sought companionship, shared common goals, and had the desire to make life on the streets more bearable. Partnering up based on common goals included travel destinations, seeking work, or the acquisition of drugs or alcohol. Given that road dogs shared the labor of survival, they typically cited that partnering up made life on the streets easier.

Loners took a different approach to survival and the formation of relationships with other homeless men. While some loners cited that they were "simply a loner" when asked why they did not partner up, most loners gave more detailed reasons. Loners frequently stated that it was difficult to find someone that could be trusted, and that not having to worry about or rely on someone else made street-life easier. For example, when a loner found a safe place to sleep, or flop, they would often attempt to keep it secret. Keeping their flop a secret allowed them to spend time in relative safety without having to be bothered by others. Road dogs also spent considerable time attempting to find safe places to sleep, however, they shared those locations with their partner so that they would have someone to talk to and someone to watch their back.

In this study, social exchange theory proved helpful in describing why two homeless men formed a dyadic relationship. Restricted exchange relationships were formed based on the acquisition and direct exchange of resources, with each partner joining to maximize their benefits. Because restricted exchange relationships typically encourage distrust and instability (Ekeh 1974), most road dog relationships were short-lived. These partnerships were referred to as road dogs for the journey. They repeatedly dissolved because of a lack of equal exchange or contribution to the relationship, heated arguments, partners possessing different goals or strategies, or because one partner found a girlfriend. When partners were able to overcome these obstacles and stay together for relatively long periods of time, they were termed lifelong road dogs.

Lifelong Road Dogs as Fictive Kin

A variety of terms such as substitute relatives, fictive kin, pseudo kin, non-kin kin, and quasi kin have been used to describe relationships resembling those of the family, but having no actual legal or blood ties. Although road dogs have been referred to as possible fictive kin relationships because "fictive" is the most popular term, the real issue is not the label. The real issue is the classification of these relationships as potential family.

Groups and individuals living at the bottom of the stratification system are more likely to rely on fictive kin (Blood 1972). It is believed that persons with greater needs are more likely to adapt to their situation by drawing on the aid of others. Blood's description certainly applies to the homeless, as the adult needs of companionship, social support, economic stability, and love were not met in traditional ways. Those living on the street were often innovative in the acquisition of those needs. With little material and social capital, the homeless typically have only others in similar constraints to turn to for assistance. Lifelong road dogs were found that lasted from approximately four months to over five years. Lifelong road dogs began as restricted exchange partnerships but over time evolved into more intimate relationships that allowed for unbalanced exchange. This reliance on others in the same precarious situation may not be the most economically productive strategy, but it does increase the possibility for relationships to form around the fulfillment of tasks typically undertaken by family members. When an individual performs functions typically undertaken by biological or created family members, they are often given the label of kin. With the adoption of the family label follow the rights, duties, affections, and obligations of real kin (Mac Rae 1992). It is for this very reason that fictive kin may be applied to road dog relationships.

Because social exchange theory did not completely explain lifelong road dogs, new action theory was used as a conceptual framework from which to view these lifelong road dogs. Although new action theory (Scanzoni and Marsiglio 1993) does not explain the formation of intimate street partnerships, it allows lifelong road dogs to be seen as fictive kin because of the numerous functions they fulfilled and because their formation was an adaptation to a lack of traditional family arrangements. Lifelong road dogs provided each other with food, clothing, shelter, information, money, protection, and emotional support. Lifelong road dogs also typically described their partners as family. In short, the label fictive kin was deemed appropriate for lifelong road dogs because they acted like kin on many levels. Used in tandem, social exchange theory explains why street partnerships initially form and how feelings of commitment are generated from patterns of restricted exchange. New action theory is then employed as a conceptual framework in which it is recognized that primary relationships may be created without institutional support.

The image of lifelong road dogs should not be one of happy homeless brothers fulfilled in their every need through permanent street partnerships. Life on the street is hard and the maintenance of relationships in such an environment is difficult at best. Road dog relationships are frequently short-lived and even lifelong partnerships can be extremely unstable during their tenure. This may lead many to ask why road dogs were examined as fictive kin rather than just friends. The answer is twofold. First, road dogs should be examined not only by what they do, but by what they replaced. Road dogs helped to fulfill roles that may otherwise have gone unfilled because of a lack of ties with families of origin and creation. Road dogs were viewed as family because they served many of the same capacities typically undertaken by family members. Second, the study's methodology gave informants a voice, which allowed for the investigation of what street partnerships meant to those involved. Results indicated that many road dogs saw their partners, past and present, as family members on whom they could rely. Even if the nature of these relationships was quite ephemeral, they served as a type of family. Rather than measuring road dog relationships by length, types of exchanges, legality, or sexual composition (Scanzoni, Polonko, Teachman and Thompson 1989), the possible formation of family among road dogs was measured by the perspectives of the informants.

Taking Action Beyond Plainview

The situation in Plainview, like all cities, may be unique in subtle ways, but the commonalities of those living without permanent shelter across the country allow policy recommendations to stem from this research.

One of the main lessons from this research, as well as from studies by Dordick (1997) and others, is that homelessness is situational. Any one single approach will not aid all those in need in quite the same way. Allgood and Warren (2003) argue that current policies that give preference to single, drug-free women with young children do not get at the core of the long-term homeless problem. Policies also need to take into account that people with particular demographic and behavioral histories, namely older men with histories of incarceration and substance abuse, are the most vulnerable to longer periods of homelessness. The case is not being made that single women and children should not receive the attention they are getting. In fact, they should receive more. What is being argued is that social service providers, city governments, and federal agencies must all understand that when seeking solutions to homelessness, the specific population must be understood. Contemporary homelessness is a large and complicated problem impacting an extremely diverse population. Given the complexities of street and shelter life, care must be taken to understand the situational differences of different categories of those without homes. Approaches to dealing with runaway youth, youth who have been thrown out of their homes, home guards, sally tramps, mission stiffs, panhandlers, day laborers, chronic homeless, those on the streets for a short time, road dogs and loners all need to begin with the understanding that different strategies may be necessary to reach the specific population.

A case for tailoring services to the population in need can be found in differences between road dogs and loners. While loners and road dogs shared many traits and experiences, their strategies for survival were far from identical. Because taking a road dog was seen by some homeless men as a strategy for survival, homeless agencies may need to address the necessities of the pair rather than those of the individual. Given that road dogs were more comfortable working as a team, the support of such partnerships may be helpful. For example, U.S. Department of Housing and Urban Development (HUD) housing vouchers are issued to either families or individuals. When one road dog becomes eligible for housing assistance, he has three choices. He can turn down the voucher and remain with his partner on the street, he can risk eviction and removal from the program by letting his partner stay with him, or he can sever or weaken his ties with his running mate. If housing programs recognized the teamwork approach to survival and allowed road dogs to apply jointly for assistance, the transition from the street to an apartment might be smoother and add stability to their lives. The added stability might potentially increase the chance that they will eventually leave the HUD housing program not because they were evicted, but because they were able to support themselves. On a practical level, considering road dogs as potential roommates would benefit the greater system by providing housing for two individuals for approximately the same price as housing one person under the current system. Loners, on the other hand, might benefit more from programs and services geared towards the individual.

Additionally, road dogs may be more receptive to programs that link individuals that have recently been housed with formerly homeless members of the community. The average stint of homelessness is approximately seven months (U.S. Conference of Mayors 2006) but most chronically homeless vacillate in and out of homelessness over the years. In the case of study informants, HUD vouchers or helpful friends or relatives sometimes put a roof over their head. However, the lifestyle transition was so difficult that many men soon found themselves back on the street. Positive mentors may help ease the transition between street life that requires thinking only for the moment, versus a lifestyle that demands planning for the future. And finally, loners in the study were more likely to state that they suffered from mental health problems. Identifying individuals who are loners, versus those who are more social, may be a first step towards determining those men who need additional mental health-related services. Loners may also benefit greatly from social skills training designed to help them learn to interact with others on social and work-related levels.

While focusing on individual-level issues and classifications may raise the ire of some homeless advocates, giving attention to problems such as mental illness and alcohol and drug problems faced in the homeless community is not victim blaming, but acknowledgement of serious issues. Individual-level problems are real and should not be ignored. Homelessness is very different than life spent sheltered, warm, and fed. Life on the street, no matter the path one took to get there, can create significant changes in a person's focus. A major problem with seeking solutions to homelessness lies in the fact that the nature of the harsh environment evokes responses to the moment, not the long term. Securing a place for the night is a necessity, but leaves little room or energy for developing and integrating a strategy for getting off the streets. The harsh physical environment, the immediate and constant need for the basic necessities of life, the risk of being robbed, and a micro economy based on cash and barter makes the prospect of individual savings quite difficult to even comprehend. As Lee and Schreck (2005) point out, the longer people spend on the streets, the harder it is for them to fulfill basic needs. As it becomes harder to meet daily needs, the homeless must eventually resort to subsistence behaviors in order to survive.

While attention to individual-level crises is important, homelessness is much more complex than the hardships faced by individuals. Understanding homelessness also means understanding the environmental and structural factors that contribute to the societal-level problem. Knowing the complexities of the homeless population can be helpful when determining what roles housed family members can be expected to play in the lives of the homeless. Although the majority of the informants in the study continually cited ties with members of their families of origin and creation that were weak or non-existent, such assumptions should not be made of all populations. The informants in the study, those living on the streets and avoiding shelters, were more likely to fall in the category of chronically homeless, thus making connections to family members more difficult to repair. Mending fences may not be as difficult with all groups. Recent research suggests that strained relationships may, in some cases, be repaired. For example, in a small study of homeless and runaway youth, Kurtz et al. (2000) found that despite the dysfunctional nature of most respondents' family relationships, in the most critical times, family members did step back into helping roles. Johnson, Whitbeck, and Hoyt (2005) also reported that about 30 percent of respondents in a large study of Midwestern homeless and runaway youth reported parents as members of their instrumental and emotional networks and over 40 percent of the youth listed other family members in that capacity.

In a rare study that followed informants over an extended period of time, Toohey, Shinn, and Weitzman (2004) argued that at the point of shelter entry the homeless women in the study likely had used up their housing support from friends and relatives. However, five years after becoming housed, the women felt they had redeveloped their relationships and could rely on their networks. Canton et al. (2005) also followed respondents over time. Nineteen percent of the sample remained homeless for the entire eighteen month study and were categorized as chronic homeless. Of those who were able to get off the streets during the study, moving in with family or friends (55 percent) was the most common method of exiting homelessness.

These studies demonstrate the potential for help from families and friends, especially among the short-term homeless, women and youth, but it is also important to remember that for some individuals, family ties will likely never be a possibility. The overrepresentation of homeless who are products of the foster care system (Courtney et al. 2001; Roman and Wolfe 1995) must be addressed. A direct strike at the numbers of homeless Americans could be made with policies that allowed for a more supported transition from foster care to independent living after a child turns eighteen.

Tailoring approaches to different segments of the homeless population is essential, but it is not the only shift in policy that needs to take place. The severity of the problem must also be recognized and more attention must be given to addressing the causes. This is a major problem that will not be fixed overnight, and will never be reduced to more manageable levels unless more focused attention is directed toward it. Those working tirelessly to help the homeless are typically doing so on a shoestring budget and with little connections to other agencies and charities focusing on the issue. Access to more resources and a greater level of inter-departmental / inter-agency cooperation would mean a giant step toward curtailing the problem. The fact that homeless men depended on each other for so many emotional and material resources illustrates what services are lacking not only from traditional family relationships, but also from agencies designed to help the homeless. The exorbitant amount of time homeless men spent seeking shelter, securing work, and finding ways to cope with their situation speaks to the deficits within the current system.

Not only is there a drastic need for services such as emergency shelters and job training, there is also a need for a change in how services are offered to the homeless population. In Plainview, like most cities, the most substantial levels of help come from agencies focusing on individual pathologies. While substance abuse and spiritual growth programs are important, men who were not in need of such services, but were in dire need of safe shelter and vocational skills, had few places to turn. The men of Plainview could turn to the city mission for a brief time but in order to stay more than three weeks, they had to enter the religious program. While staying at the mission, regardless of their participation in the religious program, the men had to be in bed by 9:00 p.m., had to keep their personal belongings under the supervision of the mission staff, and had to ask permission to use the pay phone in the lobby. If homeless shelters like the mission did not strip the independence of the residents, but instead treated homeless men like adults with something to contribute to society, the men could focus more attention and energy on the acquisition of jobs, permanent housing, and potentially even on the ties that have been severed with their families of origin and creation.

Helping people deal with job skills, family problems, addictions, and savings strategies can certainly be helpful for some homeless, but these strategies will not create a job or open an apartment that do not exist. Legislation directly aimed at issues of economic and political inequalities are needed in order to have a greater impact on the growing problem of homelessness. For example, the deinstitutionalization of the mental health care system in the 1980s is still impacting the ranks of the homeless. As President Bush's New Freedom Commission on Mental Health reported in 2003, current federal funding of the mental health system does not serve the specific needs of adults with serious mental illnesses. The current system is described by the Commission as "seriously fragmented and uncoordinated because of underlying structural, financial and organizational inconsistencies or conflicts that exist in the programs that support it" (2003, i). In order to improve the services offered to individuals with mental illnesses, the Commission recommends a fundamental transformation of the health care delivery system in the United States. Drastic changes within the overall health care system, both the physical and mental health systems, are necessary to overcome the inequalities in care as well as the access and costs to health care.

With universal healthcare far from reality, incremental steps can be taken to help both the insured and uninsured. For the homeless, the major obstacle to healthcare is access to services. The linkage between full-time employment and health coverage means that the vast majority of homeless will never benefit from coverage by private insurance under our current system. Attention to this issue must come from the public sector and be seen for what it is, a public health crisis plagued by an ineffective system. The current system is too fragmented and piece-meal. For example homeless men in Plainview were occasionally able to seek treatment for minor ailments by nursing students and their supervisors who set up clinics at The Living Room about once a month. Access to such care was hampered by the limited hours, limited skills of the practitioners, and competition for care from the other patients. In addition to these issues, prescriptions could not be written and most care focused on issues like foot care and hygiene.

The fragmentation of the system could also be found in the fact that an American Indian medical clinic was located one block from The Living Room and would see non-native patients for a sliding free. The homeless were eligible for free care but very few of them took advantage of it. Those who were new to the area or unfamiliar with the clinic's policies assumed that patients had to be Native American to visit the clinic. Shelter and clinic staff did try to publicize the fact that free care was available, but most homeless in Plainview refused to take advantage of the care. According to the staff at The Living Room, non-native shelter guests did not want to appear to be taking advantage of a clinic designed for a group to which they did not belong. A small number of informants, those also receiving Supplemental Security Income (SSI), were able to secure Medicaid but most men did not participate in the program given the obstacles for single able-bodied men, especially those transient in nature, to enrolling in the program.

These examples from Plainview are not unique. For Americans without insurance, access to care is at best difficult to achieve. The current system forces the poor and uninsured to suffer through minor ailments while hoping that they do not become problematic. When they do, expensive emergency room visits are often the only solution. Given the expense to the system when emergency room visits go unpaid, more innovative and inclusive approaches are not simply a benefit to the patients, but also to the medical establishment. Improved access will ultimately lead to a higher standard of health in the homeless and impoverished community while ultimately being less of a burden to the overall healthcare system. One approach to addressing the problem would be for the establishment of walk-in clinics designed specifically for individuals without medical insurance. In the same way that widespread immunizations by public health departments have helped to reduce childhood diseases, early attention to the sicknesses and injuries of the uninsured can reduce the reliance on expensive emergency room care and reduce exposure to the general public to diseases like tuberculosis (Wright 1990) that are far higher among the homeless.

Addressing our national homeless problem not only means focusing on the men, women, and children living on the streets, but also preventing the ranks of the homeless from getting larger. Americans who have private health insurance must deal with high premiums that are increasing far quicker than the overall cost of living. Even being able to afford insurance does not mean that one's coverage is adequate. For example, coverage for psychological issues continues to be seen by many insurers as requiring less attention than physical illnesses. As more and more Americans are priced out of the pool of the insured, or find their particular ailments uncovered, the number of people who are one medical emergency away from homelessness continues to increase.

Equally as dramatic changes need to occur within the economic sector. For Americans who are unable to work, public assistance is not adequate and difficult to secure. For those who are able to work but lack the ability to obtain a decent living wage, problems can be just as severe. With a federal minimum wage rate that is not sufficient to pull many families and individuals out of poverty, changes need to be made on a macro level. According to the U.S. Conference of Mayors (2006), 15 percent of the homeless are employed but continue to be unable to secure housing. The cycle in and out of homelessness for many individuals indicates that greater focus on the working poor, estimated to be one in six non-elderly Americans (Acs, Philips, and McKenzie 2000), would help to address problems of homelessness and poverty.

Homelessness is a complex social problem with many areas to address. However, starting with the lack of affordable housing is essential. Job training, help with addictions, more efficient social services, better access to health care, and programs to increase job development do little for someone without a roof over his head. There is evidence to suggest that this issue is beginning to receive greater attention. The United States Interagency on Homelessness has seen new energy in recent years and innovative programs are beginning to surface. Major effort by the Interagency is focused on a ten year plan to end chronic homelessness. One aspect of the program is a housing first policy. The policy, designed to target single men and women who have spent years on the streets and in shelters, has been enacted in over twenty cities. Under the program, the homeless are put directly into apartments and then attention is focused on health, addictions, employment, and securing disability or other government benefits. This program is demonstrating that addressing housing first is a cheaper system than having individuals cycle in and out of shelters, soup kitchens, jails, detoxification centers, and emergency rooms (Eckholm 2006). The possibilities of this program appear to be quite promising, but the macro level changes that need to be made in order to substantially reduce homelessness require greater national attention and resources. Two hundred and nineteen cities are participating in the ten year plan, but if only twenty cities include the housing first plan and political support for the initiatives lose steam and go unfunded, little progress will have been made in ten years.

The scope and complexities of this problem are massive. Homelessness has been a part of our national landscape from the very beginning and today's problem is larger and more complicated than ever. Given the current situation, a combination of micro and macro-level changes needs to be addressed. Individual homeless need attention to their specific problems, agencies need greater support in order to better understand and adapt to their population with greater efficiency, and societal level changes to employment, healthcare, and housing must all be addressed. A broad range of policy solutions is needed to even scratch the surface of this issue. If a multifaceted approach is not taken, millions of Americans will continue to live lives of uncertainty.

Lives of Uncertainty

I have described the lives of forty-five homeless men who have passed through or called Plainview their home. The lives of these men were characterized not only by the uncertainty of housing, food, clothing, and medical care, but also the uncertainty of interpersonal relationships. Because the interviews focused on assessing the perception that support would be available or sought out if needed, hope was a major theme throughout the interviews. Informants consistently cited that they could only hope for family support if they asked, were never sure how long commitments with their friends and fictive kin on the street would last, and ultimately, that they had to rely on themselves.

The majority of informants did not hold any real hope about support from created kin, but they were cautiously optimistic about their chances with their families of origin. Most informants stated that they had rarely, if ever, asked for support or had not totally burnt their bridges. They held on to the hope that if something even more drastic would happen to them, they could turn to their family. Ricky expressed such hope in his interview. He had lived with his sister after he got out of prison but eventually she kicked him out because of his drug and alcohol addictions. He ended up staying at a Baltimore homeless shelter for a few months before he started tramping. At the time of the interview, he was sleeping on the sidewalk outside of The Living Room. When asked if he would be able to count on his sister or father, both of whom refused to help him because of his addictions, he replied:

I don't know. I don't know. I would think I could if I was paralyzed or something. I would hope, but I really don't know. If they came to me and asked me
for help, I would be there. But I don't know. I mean, if I was helpless or something, I wouldn't have the ability to fuck myself up anymore. So maybe that
would break that tie (lack of contact).

The chaotic lives and relationships of these men were demonstrated when
two key questions were asked in the interviews. Informants were asked, "Who is
the most important person in your life?" and "What do you expect to be doing
three months/three years from now?"

When informants were asked to name the most important person in their
lives, over one-third of all the respondents and half of the loners stated that they
themselves were the most important person in their lives. These men commonly
cited that they did not have anyone they could count on or for whom they had to
care. For example, Ben explained, "Well, I don't have any kids and I'm not married. I'm not paying child support or nothing. I'm the only person that I've got
to take care of." John, who had been sent to foster care and separated from his
siblings at an early age concluded in similar fashion, "Me, because I have to take
care of myself. I'm the one that has to find the bridge to sleep under."

Many informants openly regretted or felt the need to justify why they were
the most important person in their life. In some cases it was apparent that the
informant felt they should respond that a family member was the most important
person in their life, but could not do it. DJ explained that because his parents
were divorced and he had been shuffled between multiple foster homes between
the ages of twelve and eighteen, he never developed a strong bond with his family. When asked about the most important person in his life, he explained: "I
would like to say my family is but the problem is that I can't say that because I
don't know them that well. They don't mean that much to me. They know my
situation and that is about it."

Craig, whose health was a serious concern, did not apologize for mention-
ing himself. Instead, he offered what he considered a more selfish reason. "Right
now it's me. Right now I am being selfish. I feel that I don't have that long so I
am going to do what I want to do. Because of my drinking, my way of life is
keeping me from my family. I have got some kids that are kind of pissed off at
me right now."

Of the informants that did not answer that they were the most important
person in their lives, fifteen stated that a member of their families or origin or
creation was the most important person in their lives. The remaining fourteen
were evenly split between a higher power and a friend. Six road dogs and one
loner stated that either God or Jesus Christ was the most important being in their
lives. Consistent with the theme of affiliation was the finding that seven road
dogs, but no loners, stated that a friend was the person they believed to be most
important.

Another indication of the chaos in these men's lives could be found in their
vision for the future. When asked what they expected to be doing three months

and three years from the time of the interview, informants generally expressed uncertainty. This typically presented itself in a reluctance to make a prediction. For example, Dan replied, "I don't see myself anywhere three months from now. I'm kind of a practical minded person you know. I take it one step at a time. That's good enough for me, just one step at a time." The general uncertainty seemed to stem from failed ventures. Many informants appeared to have conditioned themselves to expect failure and responded accordingly. DJ revealed his plans for the future: "Basically I am just floating because I don't make real big plans. Every time I make big plans they don't turn out. At least I tried."

The few that were able to relate a clear vision were either relatively certain they would be in a better place, or that they would be doing the exact same thing they did the day before. TC, who was married and hoped to be housed shortly after his interview, expressed clear and optimistic plans: "I want to be at least at the medium level on the income level and for housing. I want to be working twenty hours a week minimum. Hopefully, I want to be getting ready to start a bank account." Less optimistically, Trevor concluded:

> Right down here underneath the bridge. Like I said, I applied for SSI but they turned me down once. I'll be down there underneath the bridge or up in the park during the daytime or in the student union. In three years, dead I hope. I don't want to do this the rest of my life. That sounds weird but dead is dead. You don't have problems anymore. Hopefully I go easy.

The most simple, yet most poignant, plan for the future was shared by Barry, who stated, "I just want to be living like a human being. That's my goal, just to be off the streets." As Kusmer (2002) points out, the problems of people living on the street are more severe, but the homeless are not terribly different from the rest of us. Attempting to end homelessness must begin with acknowledging that reality.

Bibliography

Abel, Emily K. *Who Cares for the Elderly? Public Policy and the Experiences of Adult Daughters.* Philadelphia, PA: Temple University Press, 1991.

Acs, Gregory, Katherin Ross Phillips and Daniel McKenzie. "Playing by the Rules but Losing the Game: America's Working Poor." The Urban Institute. 2000. <http://www.urban.org/url.cfm?ID=410404> (8 June 2006).

Aldous, Joan. "New Views of Grandparents in Intergenerational Context." *Journal of Family Issues 16* (1995): 104-126.

Allan, Graham. "Social Structure and Relationships." In *Social Context and Relationships,* edited by Steve Duck. Newbury Park, CA: Sage, 1993.

Allgood, Sam and Ronald S. Warren Jr. "The Duration of Homelessness: Evidence from a National Study." *Journal of Housing Economics* 12 (2003): 273-290.

Amato, Paul R. and Joan G. Gilbreth. "Nonresident Fathers and Children's Well-being: A Meta-Analysis." *Journal of Marriage and the Family* 61 (1999): 557-573.

Amato, Paul R., Sandra J. Rezac and Alan J. Booth. "Helping Between Adult Parents and Young Offspring: The Role of Parental Marital Quality, Divorce, and Remarriage." *Journal of Marriage and the Family 57* (1995): 363-374.

Bahr, Howard M. *Skid Row: An Introduction to Disaffiliation.* New York: Oxford University Press, 1973.

Bares, Debbbie S. and Paul A. Toro. "Developing Measures to Assess Social Support Among Homeless and Poor People." *Journal of Community Psychology 27* (1999): 137-156.

Bassuk, Ellen L. and Lynn Rosenberg. "Why Does Family Homelessness Occur? A Case-control Study." *American Journal of Public Health* 78, no. 7 (1988): 783-788.

Baum, Alice S. and Donald W. Burnes. *A Nation in Denial: The Truth about Homelessness.* Boulder, CO: Westview Press, 1993.

Baumann, Donald and Charles Grisby. *Understanding the Homeless: From Research to Action.* Austin TX: Hogg Foundation for Mental Health, 1988.

Berscheid, Ellen and Letita A. Peplau. "The Emerging Science of Relationships." In *Close Relationships,* edited by Harold H. Kelly, Ellen Berscheid, A. Christensen, J. H. Harvey, T.L. Huston, G. Levinger, E. McClintock, L.A. Peplau and D.R. Peterson. New York: W.H. Freeman and Company, 1983.

Blasi, Gary L. "Social Policy and Social Science Research on Homelessness." *Journal of Social Issues* 46, no. 4 (1990): 207-219.

Blau, Peter M. *On the Nature of Organization.* New York: Wiley, 1974.

———. *Exchange and Power in Social Life.* New York: Wiley, 1964.

Blood, Robert O. *The Family.* New York: Free Press, 1972.

Boa, Wan-Ning, Les B. Whitbeck and Dan R. Hoyt. "Abuse Support and Depression Among Homeless and Runaway Adolescents." *Journal of Health and Social Behavior* 41, no. 4 (2000): 408-420.

Booth, Alan J. and Paul R. Amato. "Parental Marital Quality, Parental Divorce and Relations with Parents." *Journal of Marriage and the Family* 56 (1994): 21-34.

Bousman, Chad A., Elaine J. Blumberg, Audrey M. Shillington, Melbourne F. Hovell, Ming Ji, Stephanie Lehman and John Clapp. "Predictors of Substance Use Among Homeless Youth in San Diego." *Addictive Behaviors* 30, no. 6 (2005): 1100-1110.

Bradshaw, J., C. Stimson, C. Skinner and J. Williams. *Absent Fathers.* London: Routledge, 1999.

Braver, Sanford L. *Divorced Dads: Shattering the Myths.* New York: Putnam, 1998.

Brown, Angela. "Family Violence and Homelessness: The Relevance of Trauma Histories in the Lives of Homeless Women." *American Journal of Orthopsychiatry* 63, no. 3 (1993): 370-384.

Burt, Martha, Laudan Aron, Edgar Lee and Jesse Valente. *Helping America's Homeless.* Washington, DC: Urban Institute Press, 2001.

Burt, Martha, Laudan Aron, Toby Douglas, Jesse Valente, Edgar Lee and Britta Iwen. *Homelessness: Programs and the People they Serve. Findings of the National Survey of Homeless Assistance Providers and Clients (NSHAPC).* Washington, DC: The Urban Institute, 1999.

Calsyn, Robert J. and Garry A. Morse. "Predicting Psychiatric Symptoms Among the Homeless." *Community Mental Health Journal* 28, no. 5 (1992): 385-395.

Canton, Carol L.M., Boanerges Dominguez, Bella Schanzer, Deborah S. Hasin, Patrick E. Shrout, Alan Felix, Hunter McQuistion, Lewis Opler and Eustace Hsu. "Risk Factors for Long-term Homelessness: Findings from a Longitudinal Study of First-time Homeless Single Adults." *American Journal of Public Health* 95, no. 10 (October 2005): 1753-1759.

Canton, Carol L.M., P.E. Shrout, P.F. Eagle, L.A. Opter, Alan Felix and Boanerges Dominguez. "Risk Factors for Homelessness Among Schizophrenic Men: A Case-control Study." *American Journal of Public Health* 84 (1994): 265-270.

Caplow, Theodore. "Rule Enforcement without Visible Means: Christmas Gift Giving in Middletown." *American Journal of Sociology* 89, no. 3 (1984): 1306-1321.

Catlett, Beth S. and Patrick C. McKenry. "Class-based Masculinities: Divorce, Fatherhood, and the Hegemonic Ideal." *Fathering* 2, no. 2 (Spring 2004): 165-190.

Chatters, Linda M., Robert Joseph Taylor and Rukmalie Jayakody. "Fictive Kinship Relations in Black Extended Families." *Journal of Comparative Family Studies* 25 (1994): 297-312.

Cohen, Carl I., J. Teresi, D. Holmes and E. Roth. "Survival Strategies of Older Homeless Men." *Gerontologist* 28 (1988): 58-65.

Cohen, Carl I. and Jay Sokolovsky. *Old Men of the Bowery: Strategies for Survival Among the Homeless.* New York: Guilford Press, 1989.

Cohen, S. "Psychosocial Models of the Role of Social Support in the Etiology of Physical Disease." *Health Psychology* 7 (1988): 269-297.

Conger, Rand D., Xiaojia Ge, Glen H. Elder, Frederick O. Lorenz and Ronald L. Simons. "Economic Stress, Coercive Family Process, and Developmental Problems of Adolescents." *Child Development* 65 (1994): 1015-1024.

Coston, C.T. "The Original Designer Label: Prototypes of New York City's Shopping-bag Ladies." *Deviant Behavior* 10 (1989): 157-172.

Courtney, Mark E., Irving Piliavin, Andrew Grogan-Kaylor and Ande Nesmith. "Foster Youth Transitions to Adulthood: A Longitudinal View of Youth Leaving Care." *Child Welfare* 80 (2001): 685-717.

Deutsch, Francine M. and Susan E. Saxon. "Traditional Ideologies, Nontraditional Lives." *Sex Roles* 38, no. 5/6 (1998): 331-362.

D'Ercole, Ann and Elmer Struening. "Victimization Among Homeless Women: Implications for Service Delivery." *Journal of Community Psychology* 18, no. 2 (1990): 225-235.

Dordick, Gwendolyn A. *Something Left to Lose: Personal Relations and Survival Among New York's Homeless*. Philadelphia: Temple University Press, 1997.

———. "More Than Refuge: The Social World of a Homeless Shelter." *Journal of Contemporary Ethnography* 24 (1996): 373-404.

Duck, Steve. *Friends for Life: The Psychology of Personal Relationships*, 2nd Edition. New York: Harvester, 1991.

———. *The Study of Acquaintances*. Westmead, England: Saxon House, 1977.

Duneier, Mitch. *Sidewalk*. New York: Farrar, Straus and Giroux, 1999.

Dunn, Judy. "Annotation: Children's Relationship with Their Nonresident Fathers." *Journal of Child Psychology and Psychiatry* 45, no. 4 (2004): 659-671.

Ebaugh, Helen Rose and Mary Curry. "Fictive Kin as Social Capital in New Immigrant Communities." *Sociological Perspectives* 43, no. 2 (2000): 189-209.

Eckholm, Eric. "New Campaign Shows Progress for Homeless." *New York Times*, 7 June 2006.

Eggebeen, David J. and Dennis P. Hogan. "Giving Between Generations in American Families." *Human Nature* 1 (1990): 211-232.

Eggebeen, David J., Anastasia R. Snyder and Wendy D. Manning. "Children in Single-father Families in Demographic Perspective." *Journal of Family Issues* 17, no. 4 (July 1996): 441-465.

Ekeh, Peter. *Social Exchange Theory*. Cambridge, MA: Harvard University Press, 1974.

Elkind, David. *Ties That Stress: The New Family Imbalance*. Cambridge, MA: Harvard University Press, 1994.

Ell, K. "Social Networks, Social Support, and Health Status: A Review." *Social Service Review* 58 (1984): 133-149.

Ferree, Myra Marx. "Beyond Separate Spheres; Feminism and Family Research." *Journal of Marriage and Family* 52, no. 4 (November 1990): 866-844.

Festinger, Leon, Stanley Schachter and Kurt Back. *Social Pressures in Informal Groups*. Stanford CA: Stanford University Press, 1963.

Fischer, Claude S. *To Dwell Among Friends: Personal Networks in Town and City*. Chicago: The University of Chicago Press, 1982.

Fischer, Pamela J. and William R. Breakey. "The Epidemiology of Alcohol, Drug, and Mental Disorders Among Homeless Persons." *American Psychologist* 46, no. 11 (November 1991): 1115-1128.

Fisk, Deborah and Jennifer Frey. "Employing People with Psychiatric Disabilities to Engage Homeless Individuals Through Supported Socialization: The Buddies Project." *Psychiatric Rehabilitation Journal* 26, no. 2 (Fall 2002): 191-196.

Furstenburg, Frank F. Jr. and Andrew Cherlin. *Divided Families: What Happens to Children When Parents Part*. Cambridge, MA: Harvard University Press, 1991.

Gamache, Gail, Robert Rosenheck and Richard Tessler. "Overrepresentation of Women Veterans Among Homeless Women." *American Journal of Public Health* 93, no. 7 (July 2003): 1132-1136.

Gerstel, Naomi and Harriet Engel Gross. *Families and Work.* Philadelphia: Temple University Press, 1987.

Giallombardo, Rose. *Society of Women.* New York: Wiley, 1966.

Glass, Jennifer. "Envisioning the Integration of Family and Work: Toward a Kinder, Gentler Workplace." *Contemporary Sociology* 29 (2000): 129-143.

Goffman, Erving. *Stigma: Notes on the Management of Spoiled Identity.* Englewood Cliffs, NJ: Prentice-Hall, 1963.

Gottlieb, Benjamin H. *Social Support Strategies: Guidelines for Mental Health Practice.* Beverly Hills, CA: Sage, 1983.

Grisby, Charles, Donald Baumann, Steven E. Gregorich and Cynthia Roberts-Gray. "Disaffiliation to Entrenchment: A Model for Understanding Homelessness." *Journal of Social Issues* 46, no. 4 (Winter 1990): 141-156.

Herman, D.B., E.S. Susser, B.L. Link and E.S. Struening. "Adverse Childhood Experiences: are they Risk Factors for Homelessness?" *American Journal of Public Health* 87 (1997): 249-255.

Hewitt, Christopher. "Estimating the Number of Homeless: Media Misrepresentation of an Urban Problem." *Journal of Urban Affairs* 18, no. 4 (1996): 431-448.

Hogan, Dennis P., David J. Eggebeen and Clifford C. Clogg. "The Structure of Intergenerational Exchanges in American Families." *American Journal of Sociology* 98, no. 6 (1993): 1428-1458.

Homans, George C. *Social Behavior: Its Elementary Forms.* New York: Harcourt Brace and World, 1961.

Horwitz, Allan V. "Adult Siblings as Sources of Social Support for the Seriously Mentally Ill: A Test of the Serial Model." *Journal of Marriage and the Family* 55 (1993): 623-632.

House, James S., Debra Umberson and K. Landis. 1988. "Structures and Processes of Social Support." *Annual Review of Sociology* 14 (1988): 293-318.

Huston, Ted L. and George Levinger. "Interpersonal Attraction and Relationships." *Annual Review of Psychology* 29 (1978): 115-56.

Jackson-Wilson, A. G. and S. B. Borgers. 1993. "Disaffiliation Revisited: A Comparison of Homelessness and Nonhomeless Women's Perceptions of Family of Origin and Social Supports." *Sex Roles* 28: 361-378.

Jencks, Christopher. *The Homeless.* Cambridge, MA: Harvard University Press, 1994.

Jewell, K. Sue. *Survival of the Black Family: The Institutional Impact of U.S. Social Policy.* New York: Praeger, 1988.

Johnsen, Sarah, Paul Cloke and Jon May. "Day Centres for Homeless People: Spaces of Care or Fear?" *Social and Cultural Geography* 6, no. 6 (December 2005): 787-811.

Johnson, Kurt D., Less B. Whitbeck and Dan R. Hoyt. "Predictors of Social Network Composition Among Homeless and Runaway Adolescents." *Journal of Adolescence* 28, no. 2 (April 2005): 231-248.

Karner, Tracy X. "Professional Caring: Homecare Workers as Fictive Kin." *Journal of Aging Studies* 12, no. 1 (1998): 69-82.

Keefe, T. and R. Roberts. "Reciprocity, Social Support, and Unemployment." *Social Development Review* 8 (1984): 116-126.

Kelly, Brendan D. "Structural Violence and Schizophrenia." *Social Science and Medicine* 61, no. 3 (August 2005): 721-730.

Kiecolt-Glaser, Janice K. and Tamara L. Newton. "Marriage and Health: His and Hers." *Psychological Bulletin* 127, no. 4 (July 2001): 472-503.

Kipke, Michelle D., Jennifer B. Unger, S. O'Connor, R.F. Palmer and S.R. LeFrance. "Street Youth, their Peer Group Affiliation and Difference According to Residential Status, Subsistence Patterns, and Use of Services." *Adolescence* 32 (1997): 655-669.

Knowles, Caroline. *Bedlam on the Streets*. London: Routledge, 2000.

Kollock, Peter. "The Emergence of Exchange Structures: An Experimental Study of Uncertainty, Commitment, and Trust." *American Journal of Sociology* 100 (1994): 313-345.

Kruk, Edward. "The Disengaged Non-custodial Father: Implications for Social Work Practice with the Divorced Family." *Social Work* 39, no. 1 (1994): 15-25.

Kurtz, P. David, Elizabeth W. Lindsey, Sara Jarvis and Larry Nackerud. "How Runaway and Homeless Youth Navigate Troubled Waters: The Role of Formal and Informal Helpers." *Child and Adolescent Social Work Journal* 17, no. 5 (October 2000): 381-402.

Kusmer, Kenneth L. *Down and Out, on the Road: Homelessness in American History*. New York: Oxford University Press, 2002.

Lafuente, Corazon R. and Patricia L. Lane. "The Lived Experiences of Homeless Men." *Journal of Community Health Nursing* 12, no. 4 (1995): 211-219.

La Gory, Mark, Ferris Ritchey and Kevin Fitzpatrick. "Homeless and Affiliation." *The Sociological Quarterly* 32, no. 2 (1991): 201-218.

Lawler, Edward J. and Jeongkoo Yoon. "Power and the Emergence of Commitment Behavior in Negotiated Exchange." *American Journal of Sociology* 58, no. 4 (1993): 465-481.

Lawton, Leora, Merril Silverstein and Vern Bengtson. "Solidarity Between Generations in Families." Pp. 19-42 in *Intergenerational Linkages: Hidden Connections in American Society*, edited by Vern L. Bengtson and Robert A. Harootyan. New York: Springer Publishing Co., 1994.

Lee, Barrett A. and Christopher J. Schreck. "Danger on the Streets: Marginality and Victimization Among Homeless People." *American Behavioral Scientist* 48, no. 8 (April 2005): 1055-1081.

Lee, Eunju, Glenna Spitze and John R. Logan. "Social Support to Parents-in-law: The Interplay of Gender and Kin Hierarchies." *Journal of Marriage and Family* 65 (2003): 396-403.

Lee, Thomas R., Jay A. Mancini and Joseph W. Mexwell. "Sibling Relationships in Adulthood: Contact Patterns and Motivations." *Journal of Marriage and the Family* 52 (1990): 431-440.

Leonard, P. and E. Lazere. *A Place to Call Home: The Low Income Housing Crisis in 44 Major Metropolitan Cities*. Washington, DC: National Coalition for the Homeless, 1992.

Letiecq, Bethany L, Elaine A. Anderson and Sally A. Koblinsky. "Social Support of Homeless and Housed Mothers: A Comparison of Temporary and Permanent Housing Arrangements." *Family Relations* 47, no. 4 (October 1998): 415-421.

———. "Social Support of Homeless and Permanently Housed Low-Income Mothers with Young Children." *Family Relations* 45, no. 3 (July 1996): 265-272.

Levinger, George. "Development and Change." In *Close Relationships*, edited by H.H. Kelly, E. Berscheid, A. Christensen, J.H. Harvey, T.L. Huston, G. Levinger, E. McClintock, L.A. Peplau and D.R. Peterson. New York: W.H. Freeman and Company, 1983.

Liebow, Eliot. *Tally's Corner*. Boston: Little, Brown, 1967.

Lloyd-Cobb, Pamela and Dan R. Dixon. "A Preliminary Evaluation of the Effects of a Veterans' Hospital Domiciliary Program for Homeless Persons." *Research on Social Work Practice* 5, no. 3 (July 1995): 309-316.

Lofland, John and Lyn H. Lofland. *Analyzing Social Settings: A Guide to Qualitative Observation and Analysis*, 3rd Edition. Belmont, CA: Wadsworth, 1995.

Lye, Diane N., Daniel Klepinger, Patricia Davis Hyle and Anjanette Nelson. "Childhood Living Arrangements and Adult Children's Relations with their Parents." *Demography* 32 (1995): 261-280.

Mac Rae, Hazel. "Fictive Kin as a Component of the Social Networks of Older People." *Research on Aging* 14, no. 2 (June 1992): 226-247.

Marin, Marguerite V. and Edward F. Vacha. "Self-help Strategies and Resources Among People at Risk of Homelessness: Empirical Findings and Social Service Policy." *Social Work* 39, no. 6 (1994): 649-657.

Marsiglio, William and J.H. Scanzoni. *Families and Friendships: Applying the Sociological Imagination.* New York: Harper Collins, 1995.

Martin, Patricia Yancey. "'Said and Done' Versus 'Saying and Doing': Gender Practices, Practicing Gender at Work." *Gender and Society* 17 no. 3 (2003): 342-366.

Martin, Joanne M. and Elmer P. Martin. *The Helping Tradition in the Black Family and Community.* Washington, DC: National Association of Social Workers Press, 1985.

McCarthy, Bill, John Hagan and Monica J. Martin. "In and Out of Harm's Way: Violent Victimization and the Social Capital of Fictive Street Families." *Criminology* 40 no. 4 (2002): 831-865.

McChesney, Kay Young. "Family Homelessness: A Systematic Problem." *Journal of Family Issues* 46, no. 4 (1990): 191-206.

Mennino, Sue Falter, Beth A. Rubin and April Brayfield. "Home-to-job and Job-to-home Spillover: The Impact of Company Policies and Workplace Culture." *The Sociological Quarterly* 46, no. 1 (2005): 107-135.

Mitchell, J.C. "The Components of Strong Ties Among Homeless Women." *Social Networks* 9 (1987): 37-47.

National Alliance to End Homelessness. *A Fact Sheet for Concerned Students* 2, no. 1. 2005. <http://www.endhomelessness.org/pub/factsheets/Ushigh.pdf> (30 May 2006).

Office of the Mayor. "Mayor Releases New Homeless Count." *InterLine City of Lincoln Nebraska.* 2004. http://ci.lincoln.ne/city/mayor/media/2004/111904.htm (1 June 2006).

Piliavin, Irving, Michael Sosin, Alex H. Westerfelt and Ross L. Matsueda. "The Duration of Homeless Careers: An Exploratory Study." *Social Service Review* 67, no. 4 (1993): 576-598.

Pleck, Joseph H. "American Fathering in Historical Perspective." Pp. 83-97 in *Changing Men: New Directions in Research on Men and Masculinity*, edited by M.S. Kimmel. Newbury Park, CA: Sage, 1987.

Pollio, David. "Wintering at the Earle: Group Structures in the Street Community." *Social Work with Groups* 17 (1994): 47-70.

Pollock-Byrne, Joycelyn M. *Women, Prison, and Crime.* Belmont, CA: Wadsworth, 1990.

Powell, W.E. "The 'Ties that Bind': Relationships in Life Transitions." *Social Casework: The Journal of Contemporary Social Work* 68 (1988): 556-562.

President's New Freedom Commission on Mental Health. 2003. "Major Federal Programs Supporting and Financing Mental Health Care." <http://www.mentalhealthcommission.gov/reports/reports.htm> (8 June 2006).

Reilly, F.E. "Experiences of Family Among Homeless Individuals." *Issues in Mental Health Nursing* 14 (1993): 309-321.

Rice, Joy K. "Reconsidering Research on Divorce, Family Life Cycle, and the Meaning of Family." *Psychology of Women Quarterly* 18, no. 4 (1994): 559-584.

Risman, Barbara J. *Gender Vertigo: American Families in Transition.* New Haven, CT: Yale University Press, 1998.

Rivlin, L.G. and J.E. Imbimbo. "Self-help Efforts in a Squatter Community: Implications for Addressing Contemporary Homelessness." *American Journal of Community Psychology* 17 (1989): 705-728.

Rokach, Ami. "Private Lives in Public Places: Loneliness of the Homeless." *Social Indicators Research* 72, no. 1 (May 2005): 99-114.

———. "The Lonely and Homeless: Causes and Consequences." *Social Indicators Research* 69, no. 1 (October 2004): 37-50.

Roman, Nan P. and Phyllis B. Wolfe. *Web of Failure: The Relationship Between Foster Care and Homelessness.* Washington, DC: National Alliance to End Homelessness, 1995.

Rook, Karen S. "Reciprocity of Social Exchange and Social Satisfaction Among Older Women." *Journal of Personality and Social* Psychology 52 (1987): 145-154.

Ropers, R.H. and R. Boyer. "Perceived Health Status among the New Urban Homeless." *Social Science and Medicine* 24 (1987): 669-678.

Rosenthal, Carolyn J. "Kinkeeping in the Family Division of Labor." *Journal of Marriage and the Family* 47, no. 4 (1985): 965-974.

Rossi, Peter H. "The Old Homeless and the New Homeless in Historical Perspective." *American Psychologist* 45 (1990): 954-959.

Rossi, P., Fischer, G., and G. Willis. 1986. *The Condition of Homeless in Chicago.* Amherst: Social and Demographic Research Institute, University of Massachusetts.

Rubin, Lillian B. *Just Friends: The Role of Friendship in our Lives.* New York: Harper and Row, 1985.

Ruddick, Susan M. *Young and Homeless in Hollywood: Mapping Social Identities.* New York: Routledge, 1996.

Saegert, S., W. Swap and R.B. Zajonc. "Exposure Context and Interpersonal Attraction." *Journal of Personality and Social Psychology* 25 (1973): 234-242.

Scanzoni, John and William Marsiglio. "New Action Theory and Contemporary Families." *Journal of Family Issues* 14 (1993): 105-132.

Scanzoni, John, Karen Polonko, Jay Teachman and Linda Thompson. *The Sexual Bond: Rethinking Families and Close Relationships.* Newbury Park: Sage, 1989.

Secord, Paul F. and Carol W. Backman. *Social Psychology.* New York: McGraw-Hill, 1964.

Seltzer, Judith A. "Relationships between Fathers and Children who Live Apart: The Father's Role after Separation." *Journal of Marriage and the Family* 53, no. 1 (1991): 79-101.

Shuey, Kim and Melissa A. Hardy. (2003). "Assistance to Aging Parents and Parents-in-law: Does Lineage Affect Family Allocation Decisions?" *Journal of Marriage and Family* 65, no. 2 (2003): 418-431.

Siegal, Harvey A. *Outposts of the Forgotten: Socially Terminal People in Slum Hotels and Single Room Occupancy Tenements.* New Jersey: Transaction, 1978.

Silverstein, Louise B. "Fathering is a Feminist Issue." *Psychology of Women Quarterly* 20, no.1 (1996): 3-37.

Silverstein, Merril and Vern L. Bengtson. "Intergenerational Solidarity and the Structure of Adult Child-parent Relationships in American Families." *The American Journal of Sociology* 103, no. 2 (1997): 429-460.

Silverstein, Merril, Tonya M. Parrott and Vern L. Bengtson. "Factors that Predispose Middle-aged Sons and Daughters to Provide Social Support to Older Parents." *Journal of Marriage and the* Family 57 (1995): 465-475.

Smith, A.C. and D.I. Smith. *Emergency and Transitional Shelter Population: 2000.* (U.S. Census Bureau, Census Special Reports, Series CENSR/01.) Washington, DC: U.S. Government Printing Office, 2001.

Snow, David A. and Leon Anderson. *Down on their Luck: A Study of Homeless Street People.* Berkeley: University of California Press, 1993.

Snow, David A., S.B. Baker and Leon Anderson. "Criminality and Homeless Men: An Empirical Assessment." *Social Problems* 36 (1989): 532-549.

Snow, David A. and Michael Mulcahy. "Space, Politics, and the Survival Strategies of the Homeless." *American Behavioral Scientist* 45 (2001): 149-169.

Solarz, Andrea. "Homelessness: Implications for Children and Youth." *Society for Research on Child Development Social Policy Report* 3 (1988): 1-16.

Spitze, Glenna and John R. Logan. "Employment and Filial Relations: Is there a Conflict?" *Sociological Forum* 6, no. 4 (1991): 681-697.

Spitze, Glenna, John R. Logan, Glenn Deane and Suzanne Zerger. "Adult Children's Divorce and Intergenerational Relationships." *Journal of Marriage and the Family* 56 (1994): 279-293.

Spradley, James P. *You Owe Yourself a Drunk.* Boston: Little Brown, 1970.

———. *The Ethnographic Interview.* New York: Holt, Rinehart and Winston, 1979.

Stack, Carol. *All Our Kin: Strategies for Survival in a Black Community.* New York: Harper and Row, 1974.

Sterk-Elifson, Claire and Kirk W. Elifson. "Someone to Count On: Homeless Male Drug Users and their Friendship Relations." *Urban Anthropology* 21, no. 3 (1992): 235-251.

Stephens, Linda S. "Will Johnny See Daddy this Week? An Empirical Test of Three Theoretical Perspectives on Postdivorce Contact." *Journal of Family Issues* 17, no. 4 (1996): 466-494.

Sumerlin, J.R. "Discriminant Analysis of Willingness to Talk with a Counselor and Most Difficult Issues in the Experience of Unsheltered Homeless Men; Self-actualization, Loneliness, and Depression." *Psychological Reports* 78 (1996): 659-672.

Susser, Ezra S., Elmer L. Struening and Sarah Conovers. "Childhood Experiences of Homeless Men. *American Journal of Psychiatry* 144 (1987): 1599-1601.

Taylor, Robert J. and Linda M. Chatters. "Patterns of Informal Support to Elderly Black Adults: Family, Friends, and Church Members." *Social Work* 31, no. 6 (1986): 432-438.

Tessler, Richard and D.L Dennis. "Mental Illness Among Homeless Adults: A Synthesis of Recent NIMH Funded Research." *Research in Community and Mental Health* 7 (1992): 3-53.

Tessler, Richard, Robert Rosenheck and Gail Gamache. "Homeless Veterans of the all Volunteer Force: A Social Selection Perspective." *Armed Forces and Society* 29, no. 4 (Summer 2003): 509-524.

Thibaut, John W. and Harold H. Kelly. *The Social Psychology of Groups.* New York: Wiley, 1959.

Toohey, Siobhan M., Marybeth Shinn and Beth C. Weitzman. "Social Networks and Homelessness Among Women Heads of Household." *American Journal of Community Psychology* 33, no. 1 (March 2004): 7-39.

Townsend, Nicholas W. *The Package Deal: Marriage, Work, and Fatherhood in Men's Lives.* Philadelphia: Temple University Press, 2002.

Traupmann, J. and E. Hatfield. "Love and its Effect of Mental and Physical Health." In *Aging: Stability, and Change in the Family,* edited by Robert W. Fogel, E. Hatfield, S. B. Kiesler and E. Shanas. New York: Academic Press, 1981.

Tyler, Kimberly A., Ana Mari Cauce and Les Whitbeck. "Family Risk Factors and Prevalence of Dissociative Symptoms Among Homeless and Runaway Youth." *Child Abuse and Neglect* 28, no. 3 (2004): 355-366.

Tyler, Kimberly A., Dan R. Hoyt and Les B. Whitbeck. "The Effects of Early Sexual Abuse on Later Sexual Victimization Among Female Homeless and Runaway Youth. *Journal of Interpersonal Violence* 15 (2000): 235-250.

Uehara, Edwina. "Dual Exchange Theory, Social Networks, and Informal Social Support." *American Journal of Sociology* 96 (1990): 521-557.

Umberson, Deborah. "Relationships Between Adult Children and their Parents: Psychological Consequences for Both Generations." *Journal of Marriage and the Family* 54 (1992): 664-674.

Unger, Jennifer B., Michelle D. Kipke, T.R. Simon, C.J. Johnson, S.B. Montgomery and E.F. Iverson. "Stress, Coping and Social Support Among Homeless Youth." *Journal of Adolescent Research* 13 (1998): 134-157.

Urban Development Department, Community Development Division. *The Continuum of Care.* City of Lincoln, Nebraska, 1996.

U.S. Bureau of Census. 2000. "P39: Sex by Age by Armed Forces Status by Veteran Status for the Population 18 Years and Over." <http:factfinder.census.gov. servlet/DTTTable.html> (29 November 2004).

U.S. Conference of Mayors 2006. "Hunger, Homelessness Still a Challenge in America According to Mayors / Sodexho Survey." <http:usmayors.org/uscm/us_mayor_newspaper/documents/01_16_06/hunger.asp> (24 May 2006).

Wagner, David *Checkerboard Square: Culture and Resistance in a Homeless Community.* Boulder, CO: Westview, 1993.

Wallace, S. 1965. *Skid Row as a Way of Life.* Totowa, NJ: Bedminster.

Warshak, Richard. "Gender Bias in Child Custody Decisions." *Family and Conciliation Courts Review* 34 (1996): 396-409.

Wenzel, Suzanne L., Paul Koegel and Lillian Gelberg. "Antecedents of Physical and Sexual Victimization Among Homeless Women: A Comparison to Homeless Men." *American Journal of Community Psychology* 28, no. 3 (June 2000): 367-391.

West, Candice and Don Zimmerman. "Doing Gender." *Gender and Society* 1 (1987): 125-151.

Weston, Kath. *Families we Choose: Lesbians, Gays, Kinship.* New York: Columbia University Press, 1997.

Whitbeck, Les B. and Dan R. Hoyt. *Nowhere to Grow: Homeless and Runaway Adolescents and their Families.* Hawthorne, NY: Aldine de Gruyter, 1999.

Whitbeck, Les B., Dan R. Hoyt and Shirley M. Huck. "Early Family Relationships, Intergenerational Solidarity, and Support Provided to Parents by their Adult Children." *Journal of Gerontology: Social Sciences* 49 (1994): S85–S94.

White, Lynn K., David B. Brinkerhoff and Alan J. Booth. "The Effect of Marital Disruption on Child's Attachment to Parents." *Journal of Family Issues* 6 (1985): 5-23.

Willmott, Peter. *Friendship Networks and Social Support*. London: Policy Studies Institute, 1987.

Wright, James D. "Poor People, Poor Health: The Health Status of the Homeless." *Journal of Social Issues* 46 (1990): 49-64.

Wright, T. and P. Draus, P. "Creating Work, Creating 'Family': Homeless Placemaking on Lower Wacker Drive, Chicago, Illinois." Paper presented at the American Sociological Association Conference, Toronto, Canada, August 1997.

Yoder, Kevin A., Les B. Whitbeck and Dan R. Hoyt. "Event History Analysis of Antecedents to Running Away from Home and Being on the Streets." *American Behavioral Scientist* 45, no. 1 (2001): 51-65.

Index